SECRET SEXUAL DESIRES
OF 100 MILLION PEOPLE

Seduction Recipes
For Men & Women

Kate Bazilevsky

Demos From Shan Hai Jing Research
Discoveries By A. Davydov & O. Skorbatyuk

HPA Press

ISBN-10: 0988648571
ISBN-13: 978-0-9886485-7-9

Kate Bazilevsky

SECRET SEXUAL DESIRES OF 100 MILLION PEOPLE. Seduction Recipes For Men & Women: Demos From Shan Hai Jing Research Discoveries By A. Davydov & O. Skorbatyuk.

Editor Joice Buccarey

Book Design by Kate Bazilevsky

Cover Art by Javier Santos www.JavisArt.com

Table of Contents

PREFACE

Without the work done by Andrey Davydov and Olga Skorbatyuk (the founders of the *Special Info-Analytical Laboratory—Catalog Of Human Souls*) this book, *HPA Press* and the *Human Population Academy* would not exist. They came into being from my studies in the field of Non-Traditional Psychoanalysis, based on scientific research by Davydov and Skorbatyuk, as well as direct work with their Laboratory. I thank the scientists greatly for their research and for the chance to learn, communicate and work with them. I also thank everyone who supports the *Human Population Academy*, each in their own way.

This book is based on materials from the *Catalog of Human Population (Catalog of Human Souls)*. It is about the sexual factor of all of approximately 100 million men and women born on the dates specified. The recipes include specific seduction techniques as well as some aspects of:

❖ sexual behavior
❖ sexual preferences, desires, fantasies, etc.
❖ frequency of sexual activity, potency, preferred positions, attitude towards monogamy and polygamy, sexual orientation, etc.
❖ sexual dislikes

I must warn all readers who are astrology, palmistry, etc. fans: this book has nothing to do with astrology or mysticism. The information presented here is based on proven scientific research in the field of Non-Traditional Psychoanalysis. As for the birth date, this is explained by natural (phonological) cycles, nothing more.

If the language used in the book surprises you, you should know that it was compiled with the intent to empower everyone with the information offered. Educational materials distributed by the Human Population Academy are always presented in a style suitable for general audiences, so that any person can understand it, and *Homo sapiens* do not "remain seeds, which will never grow into trees." The *Human Population Academy*'s vision of the future is a world where every person lives in harmony with Nature and uses the *Catalog of Human Population (Catalog of Human Souls)*.

Share your journey and results of application of information presented. Your feedback is always interesting and welcomed!

Kate Bazilevsky
San Diego, California
January 2013

INTRODUCTION

How To Use This Book?

Recipes on how to seduce or otherwise manipulate you or any other person, along with information about anyone's complete psychological portrait now exist, are available and are being used. This book reveals, legalizes a demo recipes of seduction applicable to *all* of approximately 100 million men and women born dates specified. Note that recipes will work only on people of sex and date of birth specified and that differences in the sexual factor of a men and a women with the same date of birth are exactly the same as differences in the sexual factor of males and females of other living creatures present in Nature.

Whether you are gorgeous or ugly, rich or poor, young or not so young—now you can apply and test practical information provided in this book right away.

For any woman or man the given material provides recipes, formulas, and therefore an opportunity to get any man or woman born on dates specified into bed within a short period of time, and without the need to invest a lot of energy. If you happen to be married to this woman or man, you can instantly improve your sex life by implementing this information. It is a proven fact that by applying recipes found below you will make a huge impression on any woman or man born on dates specified.

If you are, know, or meet someone born on any of the dates specified below, you will now have knowledge about some of the unconscious secrets of your (his/her) sexual factor. You can then monitor your (his/her) interactions with women or men, compare with the information provided below and... well, you will come to your own conclusions.

This is your chance to match those people, who already have similar recipes on how to seduce you, and those who have similar recipes on how to seduce these and other people.

In the event that you do not know anyone or were not born on any of the dates specified, there are plenty of ways to find people born on any of these dates, apply the information provided and enjoy the results! If you look carefully, chances are that you will be able to find them not too far from where you live, in your own town. If not, do some simple research—Internet and other technological means allow you to do so very easily. You could also compare the information (or even dare to test it out) on famous people born on dates specified.

To apply the recipes and communicate successfully with people born on specified dates you will need to act. Do you remember your childhood role-playing games, dressing up, and other transformations? The recipes are scenarios that should be acted out towards people born on specified dates in order to seduce them. They should be played like roles in theater and film, or games that children play.

Remember that when you are acting out these scenarios, you do not need to be anyone but yourself. Try on a role like shoes or make-up, and remove once the act is complete so it does not adversely affect your psyche.

You will need to read the seduction scenario you are interested in provided in Part II of this book to understand the peculiarities and characteristics of the person that you will be playing, as well as likes and dislikes of the person you will be seducing. When you act out the scenario—do all the things specified in the recipe, even when it is something you would not normally do and it has nothing to do with your personal values. Use the information provided to make yourself, the conversation and the setting appealing to the person born on the date specified by implementing things from his/her preferences given in the recipe.

This is called 'transmission of manipulation (control) modes' (see Appendix for additional information). If you follow the instructions, you will be irresistible to the person born on that date.

How It Works

An image created by you that is pleasant to a person you are trying to seduce will naturally trigger a response in his/her psyche, and he/she will become more and more interested in the pleasure of your company. This will happen because you will give the person the psychophysiological pleasure that he/she needs. He/she will find himself/herself attracted to you because you will be providing that what he/she subconsciously looks for in social environments and acquaintances throughout life.

The information provided is based on unique natural psycho-physiological program and manipulation modes of people born on the dates specified. Keep in mind that the person that you will manipulate using the information provided will not be able to consciously register your actions because you will be affecting the psyche directly.

This system is now offered as a replacement for the old obsolete idea of changing the other person, which never actually worked. With this book you have the opportunity to find out some aspects of what people born on dates specified need in the sexual factor and simply give it to them. When you treat people with understanding based on new knowledge from the recipes and give them what they need (which is actually a requirement for any kind of manipulation), you will get that what you want: in this case—sex.

Other people are not like you, unless you happen to be born on the same date (taking leapness of birth year into account—see Appendix for more information). They have their own individual psychophysiology, and therefore values, desires and needs that are very different from your own. In most cases, another person belongs to another subtype of the human population. Other people are simply different, even your children, parents, spouse, etc. If you understood this, then you now know why throughout your life when you offered the other person something that you considered to be valuable, more often than not the other person rejected it: they simply did not need it because they are different from you!

The recipes provided in Part II answer the question **"What are the secret sexual desires of 100 million men and women born on dates specified?" And that, along with above instructions, is all you need in order to seduce them!** There are a lot of other recipes that allow you to do anything you want with any person, and here you get only a taste. If you are interested in further, complete information on how to control any person, how to keep him/her and then send him/her away by making him/her feel disappointed on the one hand, and with complete inability to forget you on the other hand—you can get recipes for that as well; along with detailed information on how to "tie" this man/woman to you, how to make sure that he/she sees only you. If you are interested, view and test the free demos provided by the Human Population Academy and request complete information about men or women born on any date from the Catalog of Human Population (see http://www.HumanPopulationAcademy.org). Now you can learn anyone's secrets, and use this information to your advantage by the means of professional manipulation.

It is necessary to note that people's perception of the word "manipulation" is usually mostly negative. "Manipulation of others is unethical!" you might think. However, according to the *Merriam-Webster Dictionary,* the definition of "manipulation" is simply "to manage skillfully." This means that manipulations as such are applied to objects, people, situations and more, all the time. Secondly, since it has been discovered that every person is a bio-robot with a program and manipulation modes (see Appendix), it is clear that the only ethical thing is not to break the program, not to damage a person, but rather to interact with him/her in the way that he/she needs. Also, there is nothing wrong with wanting someone and using information that is readily available to get what you want in a way that does not destroy, damage or deform the other person.

What Is The Source Of This Information?

This book is based on scientific breakthrough discoveries. Scientific research of the ancient Chinese monument *Shan Hai Jing* revealed that humans are biological machines with operating systems (human programs) implanted by Nature at birth. A long time ago, someone recorded human programs, among other information, and passed on this knowledge in the *Shan Hai Jing*. Andrey Davydov and Olga Skorbatyuk found a way to decrypt (read and translate) the information in this text. They are now compiling the *Catalog of Human Population (Catalog of Human Souls)*, which classifies every individual into subtypes and describes their psychological portraits in great detail. Human subtypes are based on phenological cycles and are identified using the date of birth.

In addition to a program, it was discovered that every human also has three manipulation (control) modes: suppressing, balancing and stimulating. Manipulation modes are correction modes of psyche and physiology of an individual. Inside of a system (a human), they act as modes of self-control which work in "automatic" mode. Being translated from the outside, they turn into a control tool, one that allows anyone to get complete power over a person. Note that intellect and consciousness of the receiver do not register transmissions of manipulation modes.

"Every person is a completely <u>cognizable, predictable and controllable</u> biological system, which can be regulated by the use of that person's program and manipulation modes. This answers the question "What is the soul?" and dismisses all myths about unpredictability and randomness of humans." Humans are programmed, one hundred percent. Whether one likes it or not, it is a fact.

It is important to understand that human programs and manipulation modes were not invented by authors of technology described above, nor the author of this book. The fact is that scientists found a very ancient source of knowledge about humans and the content of their souls (psyche)—*Shan Hai*

Jing. This text dates back several thousand years BC, and was read and decoded (decrypted) by researchers. The *Catalog Of Human Population (Catalog Of Human Souls)* is compiled based on this research and contains detailed descriptions of structures of human psyche, in accordance with the natural cycles. "*We have invented nothing and we do not invent, we simply read the text; we do not know how many millions of years old it is. And since this text—Shan Hai Jing—exists, was passed on to us by someone, left for us to study—hence, we should research it. And, if this does not happen, type Homo then remains a seed which will never grow into a tree.*" A. Davydov, O. Skorbatyuk

This research is important to every human being. The *Catalog of Human Population (Catalog of Human Souls)* could be compared to a computer operating system, the Periodic Table of Elements or the *Encyclopædia Britannica*. Whether you are a scientist, a businessman, a student, a soldier, or a housewife—no matter who you are or what you do, you can apply this knowledge and recipes in any field. Now you *can* greatly improve the quality of your life in all the factors: physical, intellectual, dietological (nutritional), sexual, emotional and environmental; because when one lives in harmony with Nature itself, all processes in that person's life stabilize and harmonize, opening up new possibilities.

In order to get a driver's license one must first go to a driving school, and then pass a theoretical test. In order to use a toaster oven one needs to know how to turn it on, where to put the bread, etc. A human is a bio-machine; psyche and physiology are different for every human subtype structure. If you wish to successfully operate and understand the needs of both yourself and others, and to communicate effectively (yes, in the sexual factor as well), then you are simply obligated to know how your machine, your psychophysiology as well psychophysiology of your partner(s) function. Information discovered by scientists and decoded into the *Catalog of Human Population (Catalog of Human Souls)* provides this information.

The Laboratory's scientific works and method are accessible via special literature about this topic (see http://www.humanpopulationacademy.org/publications/). Complete information about any person is available from the *Catalog of Human Population (Catalog Of Human Souls)*. You can also learn more about this discovery from the Human Population Academy's introductory book titled HUMAN POPULATION ACADEMY: Laws of Human Nature Based on *Shan Hai Jing* Research Discoveries by A. Davydov & O. Skorbatyuk (ISBN 9780988648500), as well as by visiting http://www.HumanPopulationAcademy.org. Human psychophysiology is very fragile! Gain knowledge on how to strengthen it.

Part II of this book provides seduction recipes from materials compiled by the Laboratory. It demonstrates manipulation tools as real instruments for practical application. Take them and apply them. Unlike some other methods, the application of information provided here offers immediate results. There is no need to meditate for years, confess your sins or seek guidance from a guru.

Techniques on how to seduce or otherwise manipulate you or any person along with information about their complete psychological portrait now exist. In relation to the sexual factor, you get a chance to consciously start a new, harmonic life with a person that you choose. People from around the world are already applying this information. Everyone should know that this information exists and anyone can use it. It is up to you what you do with this knowledge.

PART I

"Nature can exist without humanity, but humanity cannot exist without Nature."

Olga Skorbatyuk

CHAPTER 1

THE ALTERNATIVE TO "ALL MEN ARE IDIOTS!", "ALL WOMEN ARE STUPID!"

Women usually consider all men to be idiots. Ladies, you know exactly what I am talking about, and, dear men, I am sure you could not agree with me more, considering how many times you have been addressed as an "idiot" in one way or another by various women in your life (your mother, girlfriend, wife, lover, daughter, etc.). It is not surprising that men's opinion of women is not much better, especially since many women use fake, empty tricks, and actually pretend to be stupid in an attempt to get what they want. The result of this and other factors is a constant war-like situation between the sexes, not to mention lack of healthy, stable sexual activities... Why does this happen? Is this how Nature actually intended it to be, is it healthy?

Chances are men have given this some thought at times when the sexual desires are "through the roof" but you happen to be fighting with your wife or lover. Perhaps you have had to get fulfillment elsewhere due to lack of sex at home; or maybe you have thought about it when you show off in front of females like peacocks, with cars, money, clothes, family, status or strength, all to achieve a simple goal: to be left alone with a female, in order to talk about your favorite selves, the past, the future, and in the end take the woman, while visualizing someone else in her place. Consider a different example: men want and aim at becoming great. However, not all are successful. Those who fail, anyway try to *appear* as "great and mighty," instead of actually *being* that. Do you think that is attractive and healthy?

Women must have thought about this too, especially when the next macho did not get "hooked" after they demonstrated a revealing wrapping and a glimpse of what is inside by saying something like "Oh, you are so smart, and I am such a stupid woman! Come on, teach me!" While some men might find this amusing and will be happy to "teach" you right away, many think this Barbie-like approach is quite unattractive. As a matter of fact, only unskilled boys get caught this way, while men, with laughter, bypass all traps and catch you instead. If you open your eyes and take a closer look, you will see that there are smart, successful, handsome and rich men everywhere.

Here is something your mother never told you: **the principle "love me the way I am, and if not then you are a fool" does not work with men or women**. With such moves you will not be having much of a, for example, sex life (if any). Let's face it: application of techniques like this, those that were passed down from generations of grandparents and parents only introduce problems that, as time goes by, happen more and more often. Then, usually, by the age of thirty or so, everything seems already far behind. And, combined with boredom, lack of any desires, apathy, depression and complete disappointment it is a dangerous game because only a corpse has no desires, does not want anything.

It is obvious that the main cause for problems in male-female (and all other) relationships is the lack of a tool that can be used to understand and influence, or manipulate, the other person. If this were not the case there would be no problems encountered like divorce, infidelity, misunderstandings, fights, lack of sex, and many others. What is the solution, an alternative to this unnatural and damaging situation? How to have a satisfying sex life, build healthy, natural, harmonic relationships, without useless attempts at changing each other, and without lies to others and ourselves?

It turns out, there is a solution! What is it? Knowledge, of course! As stated in the *Introduction*, scientific discoveries have revealed that people are fundamentally different, and these differences are recorded! Knowledge about these differences opens opportunities to build healthy sex lives and relationships, among many other things (see the *Appendix B*). This knowledge is a tool that can be used to understand and influence, or manipulate, the other person. This means that problems of management are solved, as there is no longer lack of information on the subject. Now this information is available!

Secret Sexual Desires book provides readers with information to allow one to sample this tool. It provides specific seduction techniques based on scientific research of the ancient source of knowledge of structures of human psyche—*Shan Hai Jing*. This with data old seduction methods and tricks are officially outdated!

Those people, who already use the information discovered by the Laboratory, have a significantly higher quality of life. These people cannot be caught using the old ways, not even by a passionate, Marilyn Monroe-like performance. Using the newly discovered methods you can have as many Brad Pitts or Marilyn Monroes as you want. The *Catalog Of Human Population (Catalog Of Human Souls)* reveals detailed information about every human subtype. This information can be used to realize dreams and goals, get extraordinary pleasure and have anything you want. If you are sexually frustrated, tired of life "not working out" on its own or by the use of the old ways, if you are thirsty for new pleasure, new sensations, want to be attractive to yourself and desired by others—experiment with the information provided in this book and other information from the *Catalog Of Human Population (Catalog Of Human Souls)*. Allow yourself to try it! No one is there to forbid you.

The first step is to stop counting on old, outdated recipes on how to build your life. Secondly, it is important to feel, to be alive, sincere and honest, at least with your own selves. Remember that there is nothing wrong with admitting mistakes to yourself and to want a lot. Do not let anyone convince you otherwise if you wish to live fully, brightly, freely, passionately, and tastefully. Remember that having what you want directly depends on your desire to have it, even when you are in much doubt. If your desire to check and see if maybe, at least some dreams will come true wins over—it will pay off significantly.

It is interesting to note that obstacles to absorb new ideas do not exist for women. However, traditional male psychology, unfortunately, does not allow men to appear incompetent or weak and this often results in the exclusion of all other angles and views of the world, apart from the existing one. And, existing views, unfortunately, are not real and are only musings in the minds of men. This puts a major break on men's personal development. But that is a different topic.

CHAPTER 2

LET'S TALK ABOUT SEX:
HOW TO SATISFY *YOUR* SECRET DESIRES

Regardless of where you live and which circle of society you belong to, there are certain things that are unacceptable, certain taboos placed on sex: "Anal and oral sex are perverted!" "A woman that is not shy in bed is a slut!" "This is bad for your health!" "Monogamy rules!" Etc. If you follow some religion, then there are even more limitations placed on sex (ex.: "Sex is a sin!"). Basically, one is expected to constantly hold back, and not just in the sexual factor!

Now ask yourself: why do you have to hold back?? A human is a living biological machine that operates according to a program implanted by Nature. Therefore, sexual desires are also dictated by one's individual program. They are very powerful and it is necessary not to address them blindly. Using information presented in this book you can begin to reveal for yourself the fact that it is possible to make your sex life whatever you need and want it to be. When a person understands that he is programmed by Nature and knows his natural program and manipulation modes, he releases himself from psychological complexes that are harmful to his psyche, as well as from damage caused by society.

If you wish to, now you can stop being impacted by things that others try to impose on you and stop feeling guilty! Your "norm" is set by your program, and not by psychologists, psychiatrists, society, etc. Their "norms" are artificial and are not based on anything, except their ignorance in questions of principles of psychophysiological functions of humans.

Find out how to have sex not just in the amount, the intensity, and with that number of partners that are necessary for you to have by your own Nature, but also how to use your sexual energy for the realization of goals that interest you. Have your own norm, based on your natural individual needs instead of ones offered by society. A healthy sex life is actually one of the requirements for normal function of human psychophysiology.

And, what do you think would happen if you knew the hidden desires of your partner(s)? That is correct! They would not be able to leave you because you would have them on a leash! Why? Simply because the source of all processes in a human body (including sexual excitement) is the psyche and that is exactly what you will be influencing when applying the information from recipes provided below. "Influence on mental erogenous zones is much more powerful and effective than the usual stimulation of body parts, especially considering the well-known fact that physical erogenous zones are not universal. In other words, stimulation of a certain part of a body or mental erogenous zones, which is pleasant to one person, can cause a negative effect, loss of sexual desire and even pain for another person. Without having information about the program (or operating system) of this or that person it certainly is impossible to say with accuracy what are the demands of his or her psychophysiology. But having the data about the sexual factor of your partner (or yourself), you will not have to search for any erogenous zones because it is something that is programmed by Nature (as well as everything else) and has been recorded. So, only those, who do not know keep searching..."

Read on and put recipes provided to good use! For people born on dates specified, the information below provides a chance to understand exactly how you can be seduced, and to admit your sexual peculiarities to yourselves without feeling ashamed or unaccepted (it is ok to be who you are!). Also, if you know/meet someone born on these dates, you will now know the unconscious secrets of his/her sexual factor.

Now that you have this book with specific recipes and instructions, all that is left to do is decide for yourself—do you want to achieve results? If your answer is yes, keep reading and make sure to actually apply the information.

In order to have full control of a person it is necessary to answer two questions, "What is he like? What does he need?" In order to have a satisfying sex life it is necessary to find yourself a suitable partner using information about yourself, your natural needs and information about others. A. Davydov and O. Skorbatyuk discovered solutions to these problems, among many others. Complete information about you or any other person is available from the Catalog of Human Population (Catalog of Human Souls). Seduction recipes provided in this book are examples that you can use to your advantage and prove the validity of this information to yourself.

PART II

RECIPE 1

SECRET SEXUAL DESIRES OF MEN BORN ON JANUARY 18th OF COMMON YEARS: RECIPE FOR SEDUCTION

A man born on January 18th can be compared to a rooster in a hen house: even if he says that he does not need a 'hen house' and that he is a man of freedom, it is not the truth. He needs a 'hen house', a place or a job where there are a lot of employees, preferably mostly females. For him, it would be best if there are not too many women, but all sexually attractive.

If a January 18th born man is not married, he has many options as far as trying out his sexual strength and then choosing a life partner. If a man who was born on January 18th is married, and married happily that does not eliminate his sexual appetite, which is very original and will be discussed later on...

In the case of a married January 18th man, he can endlessly repeat that his marriage is in complete harmony and they cannot live without each other. However, when it comes to the sexual factor, this man's weakness is that he simply cannot say "No" to all other women for the sake of having just one.

On the other hand, it is possible to say that he is strong, but in his very own way. He is a strong collector: today there is one woman, tomorrow another, and the next day a different one. They are all different because he enjoys women that are unlike each other. This man is a collector who puts together his collections rather quickly and impatiently. Yet on the other hand, he thinks about his collection and may or may not like it, but he is very protective of it regardless; just like any jealous rooster who does not like competitors. A January 18th born man hates all young and old competitors alike, especially if he is the boss since he can see his employees directly from his office. As a boss, this man is actually very observant.

At the same time, his attention is goal oriented. It is not possible to just come up to a woman, make sexy eyes and expect intercourse; thus, a

January 18th born man uses multiple tools. For example, he makes up stories about urgent business trips, corporate events and parties. If a corporate party is held at a big venue or in some large building, it means that there are many hidden corners and dark places. There, unnoticed, this January 18th born man can quickly have some privacy with a 'hen' who thinks that by having sex with her boss she will go up the corporate ladder faster and get an extra bonus. More often than not, these women do actually get these extra dividends because a January 18th man is a very caring 'rooster'; a capricious one, but still caring.

Wives of men born on January 18th should not flatter themselves, even when he insists that she is the only woman in his life. If the wife of a January 18th man decides to check and see if her man is really faithful or not, she should just visit his office! If he is the boss, then she should find out for how long his employees have been working for him; ask a few of the most attractive women there how long ago they started working there. Surely, those women who have been working there for a while have not gone unattended by their January 18th boss.

When this man comes home and does not carry out his 'marriage duties', and as an excuse says that he is very tired and absolutely exhausted from work, it means that his workday or business trip included sex. It would be easy to find out whom he traveled with, and from there, female intuition will surely uncover the truth. In this situation playing *James Bond* is not recommended to a January 18th born man: regardless of how well he pretends to be a person who is always clean and always hides his footprints, he will not be able to hide from his wife or one of his lovers. Maybe he will be able to "blow dust" into the eyes of his lover, but surely this will not work with his wife.

A January 18th born man has a sharp tongue, and when he gets angry, he uses it to swear and curse. He is quite educated, or at least it would be nice if he were. However, the most interesting part is that most of all, a January 18th born man curses and swears during the peak of his sexual experiences.

A jealous wife of a January 18th born man might easily hire a paparazzi or a private detective. If he catches the January 18th naked with a 'hen', he will make sure to take pictures of January 18th's 'goods' from all angles: front, top, bottom and profile, and he will surely be caught, regardless of how he answers the "Have you been faithful?" question. However, men born on January 18th might be able to save themselves from paparazzi considering how quick they are at sex, as well as in all of their movements. If they start and finish quickly, then quickly slip out, rush to the shower and run back to work, then such "sex racers" might be lucky and might not get caught.

January 18th born men should pay attention to their shoes and to what is inside them. Yes, feet! If a January 18th uses them to simply go to work that is just half the trouble, but if he also uses them to kick around a ball, then he should ventilate his feet more often and keep his calluses under control since he not only has sex directly on the tennis court, he sometimes gets inside a bed too. Therefore, if a January 18th born man does not wish to aromatize everything around with his shoes, socks, and feet, he should pay attention to hygiene. For if he does not, then this man will have better luck with a "quickie" type sex life.

Also, regardless of his stern look, how majestically he carries himself and the delusive radiance of a crown on his head, with his love for collecting he should not forget that others might collect him too! During sex he looks good in the beginning, but not so much during the process itself, and afterwards a woman may ask herself: who had who? Then she comes to an uncomforting conclusion that she did it, not him.

January 18th's Dream Woman

No matter how persistently a January 18th man tries to show something dual, or even triple "in one bottle," women should always keep in mind that it is just a facade, a cover up. He thinks he is king and god, he is the coolest, he is the best, rules everyone and owns the world. For January 18th born men, young or not so young (it does not matter: words change, but the point is the same), he himself is the coolest of the cool.

When it comes to seducing a January 18th born man, things are quite simple. Do not be shy: what he shows (that he is great, as mentioned above), a woman should also show him. Here is exactly what a woman who likes a January 18th born man should do: she should show him that she is a woman with high standards, a woman who takes care of herself on her own, a woman that is the base of all foundations, and that she is that zero meridian from which any count must begin. This means that this woman sets the standards and is a goddess, and she sits, like a well know character from India sits on a lotus; she is pure as a virgin, has the highest demands, and if she wants something, she really wants it. If she decides that she wants a January 18th born man, it is because she has decided so, and it must be that she is turned on by the body language of this man.

This woman must let him know that she eats men like him for breakfast, lunch and... well, not for supper because by suppertime she can no longer take it, as the same thing on the menu can get boring. She must clearly show the chosen January 18th that she had men like him before. At the same time, she must show him that she realizes that he could be interesting and amusing since she is a woman who entertains herself by means of men-hunting. Moreover, she has to hint to the fact that she does not just hunt them, but she also dries and stuffs them like real hunters do. She follows the target, shoots, then stuffs, and hangs her trophy in her room. That is how a January 18th's dream woman is: she hunts like a queen and brings herself all kinds of trophies, like... men born on January 18th.

This woman comes and goes, but she constantly shows herself off everywhere she is, and at any place that she happens to arrive, she will gladly hunt down a male individual; and if there happens to be a January 18th born man, then why not? However, he must obey her, and that she must make very clear right away. Moreover, she should get angry if a January 18th does not follow her orders.

A January 18th born 'superman' is a regular man who likes to be under his wife's thumb and know his place. This wife is a goddess who orders him around, uses him and allows him to do things that she needs. In addition, she yells loudly when a January 18th born macho man does something wrong: she commands him just like a dog: "Go there! Bring this! Get that!" Moreover, this woman should clearly tell January 18th how to live twenty-four hours a day. Nothing can possibly be done without her supervision.

On the other hand, this woman should give out orders, commands, or just voice desires that absolutely contradict each other. In other words, a woman who wants to seduce a January 18th born man should even seem capricious: first, she can ask for a *Pepsi*, and after the January 18th born 'rooster' obeys this command, she can grudge and say that she ordered bananas, or coffee, but definitely not a *Pepsi*, and that this stupid man is simply an idiot who did not understand her, so he must go and do what she really wanted. Also, a woman who is after a January 18th man must be a huge music lover of quite different genres, and must constantly support this passion by offering a wide variety of music, ranging from CD's to live concerts of many different styles.

After a woman clearly shows a January 18th born man who is the boss, everything else is quite easy. After taming a January 18th man as described above, and putting him "on a leash," he will do anything: he will bring this woman things if she so desires, will carry her if needed, will be used by her as a man the moment she orders. He will undress her, lay her down, will even tell her stories if she wants to hear them. The woman should not forget to let this man know that she stepped down to him, let him be with her, touch her, and have sex with her carefully, thoughtfully, thoroughly, without being a fanatic. This woman should show a January 18th who the fanatic is.

This woman must also be creative: with all her elusiveness and royal manners, she should like novelty and variety not only in sex, so that a January 18th man will have to work hard in order to satisfy her. For example, she may demand that he becomes her servant, or on other occasions, she could demand flawlessness while wearing clothes or not, or behave as if he is wearing a tuxedo.

She might talk about her need to get married, have a family and children, yet on other occasions she might say that she needs to be free for a bit longer, and that the January 18th man must provide her with this freedom.

A successful application of this recipe completely depends on how the woman presents herself to a January 18th born man. Like any demanding queen, she should show herself as completely unpredictable and remind him of the queen from *Alice in Wonderland*: every few minutes she would yell that the person who did not fulfill her orders must have their heads cut off. It may be that the person to be beheaded did not agree with her, or maybe she just did not like them, but a woman who wants to charm a January 18th born man must behave similarly. She is not just a lady full of anger, who looks very unsatisfied—she should be explosive.

This woman should demand from all man, and of course from a January 18th man, absolute sexual variety. She gets bored doing it in the same position, or for the same amount of time every time. She wants something refreshing, yet unknown, in all its diversity. In other words, she should demand a new sexual menu from a January 18th every time, and she should create this menu herself.

She should also be in charge of the sexual process itself, but that is not all: one day, she might calmly ask January 18th if he has money. This woman may demand a suitcase full of money, and then throw it on the bed and demand to have sex right on top of it. In any case, a January 18th man will have to seriously struggle because this woman should demand that he supports her completely, and she should not allow him to get close until he shows her enough money in order to just be close to her.

This woman must be unpredictable, very hot tempered and want absolute obedience from January 18th, and all other men should be just "unidentified objects" that she will decide to try in her sexual experiments, just to see if they are all the same: maybe there are some differences?

If any woman uses this recipe to get a January 18th man, it will be tough on him! However, that is exactly what all January 18th born men like!

RECIPE 2

SECRET SEXUAL DESIRES OF MEN BORN ON MARCH 23rd OF COMMON YEARS (OR MARCH 22nd OF LEAP YEARS): RECIPE FOR SEDUCTION

Oh, two-faced demon of wild debauchery, show us your true face! Will you not show us? Well, we will do just fine without you in this matter!

Once a fine spring day, a young character from one of Oscar Wilde's books expressed a mad desire: his portrait to grow old while he would remain forever young, his handsomeness would not fade, and the stamp of passions and vices would be on the face of the portrait instead of his own. There is a portrait of a March 23rd born man, and this is his golden dream framed with stones! He really wants to stay lustrous, beautiful, perfect, a neat and compelling dandy, and try all of the dirty sins!

Look, there he is: on the outside he is luxurious, attractive, shaved, perfumed, well-groomed and radiant, a shining gentleman who is still eager to belong, or already belongs to the elite. This man goes to dirty, filthy, stinking slums of the mega-city to taste the excess of revelry and debauchery, surrounded by the smell of opium. After all, that is where one can do anything.

And, how about a dozen girls (even for money!): young, tender, fresh and innocent creatures, dolls, dressed in the style of Japanese schoolgirls—impeccably neat, with pigtails and bangs? He would love to smear them with all kinds of dirt and make them look filthy, like crap. Then, he would easily engage in wild, unbridled, blatant debauchery with them! Spending money on this is not an issue for a March 23rd man!

Oh, how wonderful it is to have fun! This man is also capable of doing the opposite from what was described above... For example, get a homeless woman covered in ulcers and sores out from under piles of rotting cardboard, pick her up from the asphalt together with her stinking, soaking clothes, then seat her next to him in his luxury car and rush off to a no less luxurious apartment. There he will wash her, clean her off, sanitize her, sprinkle with perfume, dress her like a lady, make her hair and...! Now that is a great high for a March 23rd born man!

Or, perhaps, he might choose to stay at home today and play an interesting game of cross-dressing with a friend! Oh, with what enthusiasm he will put on her clothes, lingerie and jewelry, and with what pleasure he will give her his clothes in exchange! The woman will not only get his clothes for unlimited use, but also a leash, at the end of which will be March 23rd, entirely ready to serve his proprietor and take kicks, humiliation, and a variety of mockeries.

Now it is time to travel. It would not be at all bad to arrange an outdoor brothel! Blue sea, white yacht, the upper deck is full of people: here we have ladies and gentlemen, and in the center—March 23rd, of course, as he is the greatest macho man of all time, surrounded by a dense ring of bodies of young girls.

How nice it is on long winter evenings to throw grandiose balls like in the movie *Eyes Wide Shut*; but only for his own people, the elite members of the clan, lovers of group pleasures. A rich facade of luxury, aristocratic high society, with its strict code of rules and rituals, guaranteed to ensure absolute confidentiality of the sweet process with all imaginable and unimaginable forms of perversion!

Yes, today one must pay too much for everything. Perhaps the tragedy of the poor is that they can afford only self-renunciation. Beautiful sins, just like beautiful things, are privileges of the rich. And, if March 23rd did not dig up treasures and did not get rich, then he resorts to total promiscuity, casual relations with living (and not!) objects and things. Well, for March 23rd that is not too bad either!

Particularly attractive to him are different dolls, from simple inflatable ones to representatives of the porn industry, to their most developed and advanced colleagues—robotic simulators, with a motor inside that can reliably generate practically live breath and orgasmic contraction of various orifices.

March 23rd's Dream Woman

The dream woman of a March 23rd born man has the following attitude: no man should stay indifferent to her. She will strive to achieve this by any means necessary, and for her it is not obligatory that a man is delighted after having sexual contact with her, as she finds his opinion unimportant.

Even if he remembers the experience with her as a negative one, she will not care because the most important thing is that he did not pass her by.

In sexual relationships, this woman must not have absolutely any limitations. She can try out and practice all types of sexual relations, and this includes those that are considered perversions in modern sexology and psychiatry.

Chaotic sexual contacts do not stop her from thinking about family as a must have, as she considers it to be necessary for any respectable woman. She also dreams of having it because she cannot live alone: she must always be with someone.

This woman also likes jewelry, wears it excessively and cares about the state of her nails, which is the reason she gets a manicure regularly. That is her weakness: she cannot go out without having her nails done! It is perhaps the only part of her body that gets groomed systematically, as she has a problem with hygiene and neatness in general.

She likes to gossip and discuss what is new in fashion, but she is unlikely to follow modern fashion trends, as she does not enjoy following standards.

March 23rd's dream woman also does not have any problems with appetite. She constantly chews something and snacks on regular basis, and she might even smoke while doing it.

March 23rd's Anti-Dreams

March 23rd does not like routine family life with small screaming children with snotty noses and constant colds, with countless trips to the doctor, daycare and school. The same goes for a life with a nagging wife who makes scenes and scandals from morning until night, and is capable of burying a sexually dead man right under her. Such a prospect is terribly disgusting to a March 23rd born man and pushes him to do all kinds of things.

The following joke can seriously tickle the nerves of a March 23rd born male: nice girlfriends tie him up, take whips and various sharp objects that can be used to turn a body into a bloody mess with deep scars. Then, they act out a barbaric sadomasochistic spectacle in the spirit of the Middle Ages called "castration!" The main thing here is to admit in a timely manner that this is just a joke! Otherwise, once he breaks free, the girls are unlikely to survive because a March 23rd born man does not enjoy such games.

RECIPE 3

SECRET SEXUAL DESIRES OF MEN BORN ON APRIL 6th OF COMMON YEARS (OR APRIL 5th OF LEAP YEARS): RECIPE FOR SEDUCTION

It is possible to say that the main strategy of sexual preferences of a man born on April 6th is maximum variety, constant search for new positions, emotions, sensations, avoidance of repeating, sad, monotonous, situations as well as situations limited by time and partners.

Back And Forth Looks Good In A Video

An April 6th born man loves pornography in any format: from amateur photos to different sorts and types of porn films. Actions and characters from porn films are very attractive in the sense of immediate realization of what was seen on practice. Any sexual picture gets him going very strongly, excessively aggravating his desires and sensations. By the way, this man prefers to engage in sex with lights on, so that there is an opportunity to see his own genitals as well as the genitals of his partner in detail.

What also attracts an April 6th born man is the option of filming intercourse, and viewing it on a big screen at the same time. For this purpose, a video camera gets set up to focus directly on the genitals, or is hand-held in order to not only record what is happening from the desired angle, but also to have an opportunity to switch focus to the process of recording and prolong intercourse as much as possible.

A Medal On The Penis Or A Bow On Pubic Hair

An April 6th born man can have not only heterosexual preferences, but homosexual ones as well. In the case of a female partner, an April 6th born man will suggest with pleasure that she changes her clothes, puts on a man's suit, a shirt, a tie, glues on short black moustache, and using hair gel sets her hair in place making it smooth. April 6th man will also be very happy if a woman-partner puts on a strap-on, tying it to her body with a leather harness.

In addition, an April 6th born man is very much drawn to different sorts of medals, which could hang from the neck and clink in accordance with the movements of a partner during sexual intercourse. In case of a male partner, the following will be used: red, shiny female lingerie or underpants with a sleeve for a penis, a bra with inserted silicone breasts, a smooth black wig with bangs, or a lot of elastics and hair-pins both on the head and on the pubic hair; false eyelashes, stockings with a garter belt, where it is possible to easily see naked buttocks of the partner; a silk dress or just a skirt, as a topless option. Here, hip scarves with coins could also be used, so that they clink in accordance with the movements.

Fragrant Oils Must Be Used For Massages!

The topic of massage is madly attractive to an April 6th born man as he is highly tactile, and if combined with various scents, a massage becomes twice as attractive. An April 6th born man is always interested in both his own smell and the smell of his partner: he literally sniffs her, inhaling various aromas through his nose. Refined perfumes, as well as his own stinky feet and the feet of his partner excite an April 6th man. However, an April 6th cannot stand the smell of sweat!

An April 6th man loves massage, and prefers long, painless sensations on his skin, the massage of hands, legs, back and other parts of the body; at the same time, he enjoys a massage of all erogenous zones without exception, namely his sex member, testicles and anus. However, he pays attention to how sharp the nails of his partners are and will not allow insertion of a finger with a sharp nail into his behind (anal beads will be perfect in this case).

In general, having smeared his partner in fragrant oil, an April 6th man will be happy to not only get into traditional places, but will also reach into all bends and foldings on her body: spaces between the hips, buttocks, elbow bends, armpits, cleavage, etc.

Another option for a massage session can look like this: the body of an April 6th born man gets covered in any liquor, and the massage consists of gentle biting of his body. He finds especially pleasing biting of his hips, buttocks, and around the waist.

Being a big fan of oral sex, an April 6th born man will pour liquor (especially if it is coffee or cream type) over his male or female partner's genitals with pleasure, and then he will lick it off with triple pleasure from this process.

Fine Arts

Any form of body-art stimulates the sexual appetite of an April 6th born man: painting the body of a partner, covering it with every possible tattoo and pattern, for example, using the black pencil that she uses for her eye makeup–that is pleasure! A tattoo on a forearm, a tattoo on a breast, a tattoo on the tailbone, a tattoo around pubic hair, a tattoo on the butt...

An April 6th born man is attracted to various memorable marks in general. He feels genuine pleasure while leaving traces of their rough sex on the body of his partner: bruises, burns on elbows and knees, hickeys, scratches. He is also pleased if his partner reminds him of these traces for a long time after the act. He will quiver and lovingly examine traces that were left on him as well.

This man is especially drawn to tattoos. If he sees a tattoo with his name on the body of a woman, or even a tattoo with the name of her ex, then he will become uncontrollably passionate.

Bed As A Battlefield

Fighting is one of the top favorite forms of bed entertainment for an April 6th born man! He likes to fight for anything: for the right to draw a pattern on a body first; for a side of the bed; for his own underwear, which his partner is trying to pull off; etc. By the way, any April 6th born man very much respects this attribute of his wardrobe, and usually has a whole collection of underwear. He also pays burning attention to the lingerie of his partner. An April 6th prefers to see something new, beautiful, fashionable every time, and especially likes to see scarlet-colored lingerie.

This man certainly enjoys fighting during sex itself: who gets to be on top, who will exhaust whom, or who will set the friction rate. There is also the fight for the duration of the sexual intercourse: at the moment when his partner is close to orgasm, he can suddenly pull out in order to delay her happiness as much as possible. An April 6th born man is not opposed to this being done to him as well.

Here, a "rape" game is also desirable: I try to grab you and you resist, or the other way around. Also, there is the "catch-me" game: you escape, and I shall catch you... but you slip out and escape again, and I shall try to catch you again...

Get Naked And Prepare The Instrument!

An April 6th born man is capable of testing very strong sexual sensations, for example, in the following situations:

- ❖ Engaging in sex within space limited by a paling from double-edged swords. The risk of feeling pain, brushing against a sharp edge of one of the swords in a fuse of passion brings him unbelievable sensations.
- ❖ Engaging in sex on a bed that has sharp edges and peaks along the perimeter.
- ❖ An opportunity to be in the role of a target for a knife-thrower.

In other words, any anticipation of getting hurt by a sharp object causes a sharp attack of excitement in an April 6th born man. He is excited by the prospect of walking barefoot on beaten glass or laying down on it like a yogi.

A gunshot is another thing that makes an April 6th born man get unforgettable feelings that surpass all his previously experienced orgasmic sensations. For this purpose, both a banal New Year's firecracker or a blank gunshot can be used. However, he will have true and incomparable pleasure if a real weapon is used (a shotgun, a rifle, etc.).

Goo Goo Ga Ga

A man born on April 6th has a passionate desire to literally swaddle his partner. Any blanket will work perfectly for this procedure. He will kiss his "baby" with delight and affection, will swing her in his arms, and then undo the bottom part of the envelope, and... well, you understand.

This man also finds the idea of engaging in sex in a sleeping bag quite attractive. Very little space, a lot of sweat and wet slippery bodies will create an additional element of fun for this man.

Also, with age, an April 6th born man can begin to be drawn to young and tender individuals.

Getting Caught

This man finds all sexual situations where it is possible to get caught highly attractive. Such prospect pleasantly tickles his nerves and adds a special, delicious flavor and spice to intimate relations. His favorite places for this are beaches, where one can remove all clothing and make love in the dunes or on the sand right by the water, especially since a tropical beach is the place where this man feels most comfortable in the male role.

Swimming pools, lakes, seas and oceans are attractive places to engage in sex to an April 6th born man. The same goes for a "sudden" audience, as it increases his desire and feelings.

He is also not against vehicles of different kinds, such as a car with untinted windows, which will swing and sway to a point that not only people passing by will pay attention, but also half of the district will come to watch.

Another favorite is an airplane, where it is possible to sit his beloved on his lap, cover up with a blanket, and indulge in amorous pleasures next to neighboring passengers who are "fast asleep" from embarrassment. Or on a train, where someone can come by at any time. It may also be a hospital room that someone forgot to lock; or an empty classroom; or the bedroom of a party host who is busy with celebrations; or a public women's bathroom; or even a banal situation of "we were not expecting you" in his own apartment, involving, for example, parents who "decided to suddenly drop by."

Just Keep Talking!

April 6th born men like to talk in bed, before, during, and after sex, and especially enjoy the dialogue or monologue of the partner. The following are some of the topics for perfect conversations:

Before: an active exchange of news and events from different areas of life.

During: heated fiery speeches about love and passion; about how he is unique, irreplaceable and how "the soul comes apart" during partings.

After: any stories in a whining manner about troubles and vicissitudes of this imperfect world, or this cruel society.

A Mountain Of Beautiful Bodies!

Perhaps an April 6th born man invented swinging... He enjoys group sex, where it is possible to see the real-time grand porn movie, get a lot of tactile sensations that are so pleasant and desirable to him, and be in the nude, naked in front of everyone. It is also an opportunity to get pleasure from sex by employing all of his erogenous zones: oral, anal, regular sex with men and women—what could be better?!

Group sex, absorbing the maximum amount of this man's sexual preferences, can outshine all the other ways of getting pleasure, and if the partners will be living embodiments of beauty, all with beautiful, perfectly tanned bodies and white *Hollywood* smiles – that would be best! Oh-oh-oh-oh, what a dream!

April 6th's Anti-Dreams

An April 6th born man hates dystrophic women, creatures that can easily be used to study anatomy. He cannot stand long pubic hair and "vegetation" under the armpits. The image of a woman getting out of a pond while being completely covered with long weeds, caught in her long pubic hair, can completely discourage any sexual desire in an April 6th born man.

Never offer him to play "horsey," especially as an ultimatum, or in a rough, dictating form. Also, do not offer to put him on a leash or play some other animal that gets trained using "first a carrot, then a stick" approach. A commanding shout, such as "drop to your knees and pretend to be a horse, or you won't get any hey today" could be the last in your life.

In general, being ordered around, or playing a mat on which one wipes their feet on is unacceptable to April 6th. The role of sexual object to satisfy the sexual needs of ladies, or doing it during his lunch hour every day from noon to one is completely intolerable.

Any scheme like "I am the boss, and you are the fool," with replicas such as "Listen here, I'll tell you how and what to do, and hurry up, come on, I'll be late for work" will end badly, to put it mildly. Do not offer the same "professional" versions of sexual games of disguise, such as wearing a business suit or a nurse outfit. This man does not like to have sex in clothes. He also hates amulets and charms of any kind, as well as women who perform rituals prior to sexual intercourse.

He has a very negative attitude towards anything funeral related, so do not offer this man to have sex in a coffin, or surrounded by artificial flowers while wearing white slippers.

He cannot stand the perspective of getting burned: at the mere sight of candles, especially the silver-gray colored ones, this man can be unpredictable in his anger.

Also, an April 6th born is annoyed at the slightest hint of a religious robe and icons in gold with stones. In small doses they can cause an attack of unbridled debauchery; however, in large doses, they will cause a sharp rejection.

RECIPE 4

SECRET SEXUAL DESIRES OF WOMEN BORN ON MAY 28th OF COMMON YEARS (OR MAY 27th OF LEAP YEARS): RECIPE FOR SEDUCTION

May 28th born women are very interesting. She reminds of great architecture, something that has already been completed and is about to be presented to tourists, or is about to be exploited. She is absolute perfection, completely unapproachable, downright amazing and very professional. A May 28th born woman is complete, autonomous, and knows and understands things clearly. At first glance that is...

If one happens to see her in a private setting, then one would find out many interesting things. For example, in spite of all of her attempts, she is not always able to control her emotions. However, most of the time she is in and about control, more control and a bit more control. The result is always the same—success. In other words, emotions always work, and are always being controlled.

However, situations can be different, life changes often, and sometimes it can be fast-paced and wild. Certain situations can make a May 28th born woman angry. Then, she shows an attitude filled with prejudice and makes caustic remarks. If she happens to be a big boss, she can even force others out of their comfort zone. If she does not stop at the right time, she will become so ferocious, so emotionally distressed that she will actually become unstoppable, and then, she might not always be fair.

What does this have to do with the sexual factor of a May 28th born woman? Well, here is what is interesting: when a May 28th born woman experiences emotions like anger and outrage, she shows fantastic sexual excitement, and this sexual tension completely absorbs her and everyone around her, all of those who she calls by different names!

Moreover, a May 28th born woman has a certain particularity: her emotional outbursts do not just make her act in harsh ways, but make her sexually attractive as well. If one has a verbal fight with her in the morning or in the evening, she will be very interested in sex both in the morning and in the evening. At the same time, she will keep fighting, yelling, and, as she likes to say, she will "not be in a very good mood." In the case of May 28th born women, sex begins with a fight!

A May 28th born woman is serious. Although she sees marriage as a positive thing, she does not enjoy living on someone else's money. What she does like is being the jealous mistress of the house. If a May 28th born wife becomes suspicious that her husband is having an affair, beware, for there will be no end to her jealousy, and in that respect she can be quite scary.

She is also very independent, so much that she reminds one of a cat. Considering the fact that this woman strives to be a professionally accomplished woman, she can successfully manage to use her professionalism in her sex life as well.

Everyone who dreams of reaching the top is interested in knowing the recipe on how to actually do it. In the case of this woman, she has it, and in that she is not original: when it comes to manipulating the male individuals that she comes across while trying to reach her career goals, this woman will use sex. Since she is not stupid, her managers will be in luck. She will not be a burden as far as her sexual relations with them, but if those managers do not keep their promises, they will find themselves in a bad situation...

As mentioned above, a woman born on May 28th is a smart woman and she enjoys learning and discovering new things. She wants to gain practice in many different fields, and is quite lucky in that she completely lacks the feeling of being a novice. This helps her quickly become a professional in anything, including sex. It is very unlikely that she will not choose sex in addition to everything else as a field in which it is desirable to be a professional.

As the sexual experiences of a May 28th born woman further, she can, in turn, become a very good teacher for men, and, of course, her husband will not be bored with her. On the one hand, this woman is not against marriage and children. On the other hand, she is not against making a solid career, as mentioned above, so it seems like everything about her is quite ordinary.

However, there is a certain aspect to a May 28th born woman. This side is well hidden, and it is unlikely that she wants this side of her to be seen. The fact is that her sex life is like two sides of the same coin. One half is similar to a life of a good schoolgirl, or even a well-educated nun, who on weekdays is completely oriented towards making a career and accomplishing things related to her professional life, as well as complete independence from everything.

The second half of this woman is very interesting. She can easily be called a sexual revolutionary, or even a sex advocate. Moreover, a May 28th born woman participates in the wildest sexual experiments, and can carry out any sexual fantasies.

In other words, one side of the coin is official and "buttoned up," while the other side can warm up the palm of one's hand so much, and stir up such sexual desires that a man can only dream of.

May 28th's Dream Man

If a big military man meets a woman born on May 28th while she is vacationing and becomes interested in her, he should consider it thirty percent done! However, if he does not have a goal in life, and goes from one thing to another, unable to choose, it is best to not even approach her. A man who wants to seduce a May 28th must be clear about what he wants. Military men usually have this understanding: they know what the target is, know the enemy and the goal, so for them there is nothing to be unsure about, and a woman born on May 28th clearly understands that here is a holistic, goal-oriented man.

A military guy should be smart and a good thinker. He should not only be educated, but also wise and knowledgeable enough to have his own opinions. That is necessary to charm a May 28th born woman because one needs to "have a brain" in order to do so. You need to be able to carry a conversation, at least during the initial stages of seduction.

A May 28th born woman likes to talk, and not just to talk, but to discuss many different topics. Here, a *Navy* or an *Air Force* man should show himself and entertain her with various topics such as culture, theater, opera, ballet, etc. And, of course, it would be best if the man is not simply able to hold a conversation, but also looks according to his military status, or at least looks like he can be in the military because he is well trained. He must enjoy all types of male sports and his looks must show it!

In other words, to charm a May 28th born woman, a man should have a smart appearance, as well as muscles. At the same time, he should be very flexible. He must also know how to dance, be very good at it and actually enjoy doing it. If this man happened to not only be in the military, but also a professional dancer, or a man who takes his dancing hobby seriously, he will score even more points with May 28th because it is very unlikely that she will turn down an invitation to dance. However, she will accept this invitation when the setting, the situation and the right time come.

Of course, the situation should change after the initial few minutes of them becoming acquainted: separate sentences should turn into specific offers, and afterwards, if the man suggests that the two of them should meet up and gets a "Yes" out of her, he will have a chance for even more points.

If during the first meeting with a May 28th born woman a man wears a strict, military-like uniform, then for the next one he should show up in something very different, something in which he can shine. In any case, there is no need to restrict his choice of colors, and it is even possible to look like a rainbow, as long as he does not appear untidy. His look should be based on works of art, designer masterpieces. If this man does not know any, he should definitely check them out if he is looking to seduce a May 28th born woman. If he is not only creative, but also a good singer (in addition to being a good dancer), then consider those points to slowly but surely be rising to one hundred. There is very little left after this.

In order to score one hundred points with a May 28th born woman, it would be a good idea to ask her out to dine at a restaurant. She will be very pleased to hear a man say that he enjoys good restaurants and visits them often. Also, this man could tell her that sometimes he likes to experiment and have fun with cooking, as she will like that as well. However, be careful— when he invites her over, this man will have to cook something because if he says that he can do something, he also needs to prove it. After he invites her to his home or to a restaurant, it would also help him to have some knowledge about wines and be able to easily talk about them. When, where, what and by whom was a certain wine made? What is the difference between this wine and that wine? What type of wine goes best with which dish?

If a man sets his mind on seducing a May 28th born woman, he should also mention that if he had a big enough house he would be more than happy to have a large wine cellar, and in this cellar he would not only have wines that were just bought yesterday, but also wines that he would hold for special occasions. And, of course, an evening with a woman like a May 28th is a special occasion! In that case, he would definitely have to open the most expensive bottle of wine from his cellar, just for her! Cheers to a wonderful evening! To a dream! To the future!

A man should show a May 28th born woman that, independent of all his masculinity and goals, he is in fact very soft, optimistic, understands family relations and how to be with a woman. At the same time, he must show great emotional fireworks. In other words, he must have these emotional fireworks spontaneously. For example: "Oh, how wonderful you are, May 28th!" or "What a perfect evening!" or "I am so afraid this evening will be over!" In other words, a man should not be scared to show a soft side, especially if directed at the May 28th born woman, for when he shows this, he can rest assured that this woman will enjoy it. If during a dialog with her he makes sure to include something from deep within his romantic fantasies, he will get his desired one hundred points with her.

As far as his romantic fantasies this man should say that he sees his future only with this May 28th born woman, that she should be with him and that he envisions their life together with nothing but bright blue skies, sunny days, flowery fields, a good financial base and stable future. In other words, he sees his life only with her and no one else, and it is absolutely perfect.

After this, there isn't much left to be said, and all he needs to tell this May 28th woman is that he never met anyone like her before and that he never, ever experienced emotions like he does now when he is near her, that this meeting is out of the ordinary, and if it never had happened, he would consider his life worthless. He should also mention that if he finds out that she wants to get married, he will make every effort to make her his. After this, the man can go ahead and grab his remaining few points. He must not only be detail-oriented, romantic, and giving, but also daring. He should boldly "attack" the chosen May 28th woman after creating situations and doing things specified above.

At this point, he should tell her about his feelings straight, and make his proposal once and for all. He could propose different things: for example, a hotel room, but if he and May 28th are already in a room at home, then the man should suddenly offer her to go to the bedroom "before he explodes." If not very sure whether he is a sex stayer, then he better not try to do it with May 28th born women; moreover, if as a sex partner all he can offer a woman is two basic positions, and nothing out of the ordinary, nothing interesting—she will be greatly disappointed, and the chances that she will want to do it with him again will be very slim. Or, if everything is OK and this man is good in bed, at some point he should mention that he is extremely jealous, and is not against marriage and children.

When using this recipe to seduce any May 28th born woman, men must think before they act. If instead of a multi-page emotional menu all he has is gum, he better not approach a woman born on this day. If he does try everything specified above, but in reality he is not so good in bed, this man should beware, for a May 28th woman will find a way for cruel revenge. The man will get to sleep with her, but her revenge will be thorough, so he better wear some metal underwear...

RECIPE 5

SECRET SEXUAL DESIRES OF WOMEN BORN ON JULY 6th OF COMMON YEARS (OR JULY 5th OF LEAP YEARS): RECIPE FOR SEDUCTION

Men, consider yourselves lucky if you meet a woman born on July 6th. It is impossible to say that this woman just likes sex: she absolutely loves it! But there are certain particularities, as women that were born on July 6th are not always like this. However, they do get wildly passionate quite regularly, and they are ready to do anything in order to fulfill themselves.

Their sexual excitement is at times so high that it simply must be discharged, as otherwise, this woman will behave very strangely and an ambulance will have to be called in order to calm her down. It would be great if there were some cute paramedics that would understand the problem and help her out. They should be able to choose the treatment correctly. In any case, if everything is OK with this woman's arms, legs and body, and she already has legal documents from her country of residence, then they will manage to find common ground. Everything will be just fine. The only problem is that the paramedics may be helping her for quite a while because for a July 6th born woman it is impossible to have sex for only five minutes, and the longer and deeper the treatment, the more effective the result will be, and the recovery rate will be much greater. So, the longer the time is spent on the treatment, the better the health condition of the July 6th born female patient.

If we remind ourselves that paramedics are people who actually take the initiative and that is why they get called in the first place, then another side of the question will also be answered: July 6th born women like men who take the initiative themselves. Men that draw circles with their feet do not really interest her. July 6th born women like quite the other type—the ones who provoke, entice, charm. Those men can expect quite a stormy response.

So, dear men, the type of response that you will get from July 6th born women depends directly on how you ask "What do you want?" Do not mumble, talk about work, your bright plans for the future, etc. July 6th born women will not understand that. She will think to herself: "I am here now and this guy is talking about some far away prospects that are not even mine, but his own! I do not need this!"

Men, be careful: if this woman set her eyes on you, it is possible to say with confidence that you are doomed, and do not even hope to avoid contact with her. She is a type of woman for whom, once the goal is set and gets planted firmly in her head—that is it: she will give herself completely in order to reach her goal. In this sense, she clearly understands that either she gets the result or... she gets the result. And, in that sense, she is absolutely merciless!

Maybe those men on whom July 6th born laid her eyes will still want to try to escape her. Well, then you would have to run to the penguins, but even then it is not possible to guarantee that July 6th born woman will not find you there.

Let's say you met a woman born on July 6th and you are not a very brave man, but you are interested. If she sees that you are about to run far and forever because you simply cannot handle the pressure, then she can trick you very dashingly! She can appear so calm, indifferent, unexpressive, boring, and ordinary that you will not be able to understand why you were so afraid of her. Everything is cool right here! You will not remember why you had the idea to run away, and you will begin to feel friendly towards this woman. At that point consider yourself caught because this woman is absolutely polar-emotional: first she can be as cold as ice, and then passionately wild like a gas-stove.

So, guys, if you get caught by July 6th's "complete indifference," then you should understand that next, she will make a barbecue out of you. It will already be too late when you remember yourself after all these passionate emotional changes: you will get used as designed. Well, maybe not by your design, but by the design of this July 6th born lady, and the score will not be yours anyway...

However, do not be sad, for a July 6th born woman is ruled by her mood; maybe it happened that you were looked at as an exotic, sexual male and it was necessary for her to get familiarized with you in order to try you out, so to speak. Are you tasty or not? There is no need to ever try again... with you that is. Therefore, later on, she might say: "Yeah, I tried him. Such a boring individual!"

On the other hand, if you are still upset, do not be. Perhaps, you never had a woman like this before and maybe you never will again. It is possible that you may not ever see such a sleek, well-groomed, spectacular woman after that. Well, you will see them in glossy magazines, but it will not be possible for you to touch, so you will be left with a bunch of papers in your hands. So, do not be sad, after parting with a July 6th born lady. Instead, consider yourself lucky!

This woman is quite fascinating. Sex, power and money–that is a very interesting combination. And, if in a country where sex stands before power and money, then a July 6th born will try to make her way to the top of the power pyramid using fire and a sword. Power will be used to fulfill her most unbridled sexual fantasies. Perhaps it might be interesting to participate, if she allows of course...

Men out there who want a July 6th born woman should be warned: you have two options. Option one: you spend money on her, and quite a lot of it. Option two: you do not spend any money at all. Of course, it is preferable to not spend any money, but then you will have to take her to parties, and wait for the right moment and make sure that some time has already passed since this July 6th born lady joined the party. Of course, you should also keep an eye on how much she had to drink since July 6th born are not against drinking.

You should keep track of what and how much she drank, and see if she already poured enough strong and tasty cocktails into herself. If that is not the case, then it would be good for you to pour her and yourself some more alcohol, and make a toast. After that, you are almost done. If you make sure to keep watching that her glass is not empty, then in the morning you and July 6th will wake up looking into each other's eyes.

If you do not want to wait, and prefer to take and control the whole process fully, then first check your bank account to see how much money you have: July 6th may stun you with her complete elusiveness when you look at her from a distance, and then your belief in the amount of money that you have may be shaken.

However, if you are a man who chooses the path of using the recipes of how to seduce July 6th born women, then first of all, you must be a very good thinker who considers and analyzes very quickly, and has great attention to detail. This person collects recipes for seduction, and that reflects in the way that he carries himself. And, of course, when talking to a July 6th born woman, this man must first show interest in HER. He should not present himself and explain how great he is, but instead, he must be fully focused on the July 6th born woman and ask her questions like: "So, where does such a lady come from?", "How did you get here?" Also do not forget to ask if there is a chance of meeting her.

July 6ᵗʰ's Dream Man

Prior to talking to a July 6ᵗʰ born woman you should look at yourself in the mirror. Many men out there think that they are perfect like a present. However, a man who is interested in successfully seducing a July 6ᵗʰ born woman must really look physically perfect, not just because he looks that way naturally, but rather in comparison to other men. He must go to the gym regularly, if he takes his shirt off at the beach he must look like *Apollo*: there must not be any fat at all and a sculptor should be able to use him as a model. That is how a man who is trying to get a July 6ᵗʰ born woman must look.

If you are in a place with this woman where you cannot undress completely and demonstrate all your goods, then pay close attention to your appearance: there is no need to put on make-up and dance in front of mirrors, as that is quite a different story and does not apply to the seduction process of July 6ᵗʰ born women; however, you do need to experiment with how you present yourself, and specifically with how you present yourself to women. This is the kind of man that July 6ᵗʰ born women like.

The man must be able to experiment and combine many different styles in order to find his own. To make sure that he is seen from a distance, he needs to show that he walks, talks and presents himself as someone extraordinary, a stylish, original man who knows how he should look, a man who takes care of his body and the packaging. His main concern should not be about being like other man, but rather he should strive to be exclusive. So, guys, if you have no problem with body fat and appearance, then it is time to talk about what kind of offer you can make in order to seduce a July 6ᵗʰ born lady.

First of all, you must clearly understand whether you are a sprinter or a stayer. In other words, a man who is interested in getting acquainted, seducing, doing their thing and running away quickly should not even bother trying to seduce a July 6ᵗʰ born woman. This woman likes to take time to meet you, take time in the seduction and, of course, take time throughout the whole process itself.

This woman likes men and gets completely charmed by those who can do it for a long time, many times, in a tasty way, and with pleasure. You should offer to go for a very nice and tasty dinner, argue with the waiter about the wine in a calm manner, and then order the best food and wines without the help of the waiter. Moreover, this man, as a regular of fashionable restaurants, should demand the top-notch quality of everything in front of him with ease. He should invite a July 6ᵗʰ born woman and make sure that it is not just a food consumption type of event because a July 6ᵗʰ born like to take their time and do not enjoy any fast foods. This woman wants not just a dinner, but more like a high class dinner and a show; not simply a good restaurant, but one that provides an original menu, exotic foods and cuisines. That will really work on her heart. Well, maybe not her heart, but her stomach, and as you probably know, the way to a woman's heart is through her stomach.

In the process of such communication the man should be a professional seducer, know exactly what he is talking about, be well-educated, with solid intellectual abilities. He must also be a hunter, who hunts original women as "a cannibal who collects heads." He should be patient, be able to wait, charm, try and experiment with what a woman born on July 6th reacts to, to what words, emotions, eye expressions she responds.

Do not forget to hint that you are not at all a young boy as far as intimate relationships go. Quite the contrary, you should present yourself as a professional who can do things that are not written in books, and do not even mention what you read about sex in popular magazines.

So, in order to get a July 6th born woman the man must be original not only in what was mentioned above, but he should also be original in sexual contacts and relationships. And, he should be interested in sex. He should be even more interested in special things, new things, something absorbing and interesting, and even better, something that cannot be repeated. He himself should be ready with many sex recipes. As a high-class cook in an exclusive kitchen, he should mix sexual aromas; make something extraordinary in taste, smell and presentation during sexual contacts. He should be like a sex-cook with a great kitchen. To make that happen he should use his fantastic ability to act: be ready to play any role, and much better than actors of *Stanislavsky*'s method. He should hint to a July 6th born woman that other women like him especially for this, and that they do not try to cut off the relationships after trying out his recipes.

Make sure this July 6th woman clearly understands that you are for real, have sex recipes, and might use them, or not. In any case, make sure to let her know that you are very interested in her, but also ask her what she can do. Basically, suggest that you have women to experiment with and ask: what about you, July 6th? What can you do? Then, this woman will definitely like to compete with such a man. July 6th will think to herself: "We will see which one of us lights up the sex diamonds instead of stars in the sky first! We'll see who knows the subject better!" As soon as you see or feel this type of reaction from a July 6th born woman—consider it done.

Therefore, all you have to do to get any July 6th born woman is use the recipe above and not lose face once you end up in bed with her!

RECIPE 6

SECRET SEXUAL DESIRES OF MEN BORN ON AUGUST 2nd OF COMMON YEARS (OR AUGUST 1st OF LEAP YEARS): RECIPE FOR SEDUCTION

The following information will be especially interesting to women who like strong sensations, adventures, passion, sobbing, and more. An August 2nd born man is quite spontaneous: first he laughs, then he cries, and then he makes declarations of love. He is romantic, and then he is suffering deeply. Suffering from... well, just suffering, just because he wants to.

A large audience stirs up special feelings and sensations in an August 2nd born man, especially a female audience. In this situation he will be absolutely unstoppable and tirelessly keep presenting himself as fantastic and outstanding. Of course, his main goal is to charm, and that he does successfully. He seems as an interesting person to women. He has no limitations.

As far as the sexual factor goes, this man is very original. And, by the way, dear women, August 2nd born men are not cheap. A male representative of this subtype structure is ready to charm a woman by spending his last money on her: he would do that for his own pleasure, as well as for the sake of the process of charming and the process of flirting itself.

There is never too little of him, as there is always a lot of him. He is very joyful, or he can be very joyless, but he likes sex regardless. This is likely to be good news for women who are looking for sex adventures. By the way, there is no need to worry about his hygiene because August 2nd men are always clean, fresh, cheery—always ready to service women.

As far as intimate relations go, he can play anyone for you. He has great acting abilities and he is ready to pleasure a woman. He is sensitive to a woman's wants. Many people act and want to be in the movies, many want to become famous and popular, make it to *Hollywood*, etc. An August 2nd born man wants to charm women.

Sex is probably what attracts him most and he is ready for anything. He will make any dream, create any image for a woman. He will realize the most daring fantasies. An August 2nd born man likes to fantasize as well, very much. Realistically, he is ready to realize even the deepest sadomasochistic desires of a woman, though he naturally has his own limits.

However, he does not stop after one woman, and of course, there are many women. He knows this, and he charms one after another with pleasure. It is possible to say that in sex he really is tireless. An August 2nd born man can do it fast, and can do it anywhere, but he especially enjoys doing it in a swimming pool or in a jacuzzi. That of course, is a special preference of his.

He particularly prefers for the jacuzzi to be located in a splendid house with a nicely made interior. In that kind of surrounding he will perform one hundred percent! If women out there think that this man will somehow not satisfy them, they are deeply mistaken. An August 2nd born man is astonishingly creative when it comes to women, as he can adjust to anyone. That is one of his particularities.

If a woman needs "a ladies' man," he can do that; if she needs a dedicated dog type, no problem. If she needs a scary macho man with shinning eyes—August 2nd is ready to play that too, and he will become so carried away that he will actually believe in the role that he is playing.

Yes, August 2nd born men really are like that: they can change quite surprisingly. They are ready to satisfy any desires, ready to do anything in order to get sex, and with August 2nd born men, sex can be very wild. However, there is also the following aspect: if this man gets access to the body he can become completely unstoppable, and hug the woman so passionately that she may want to think about protecting her skin. Of course, if you are one of those women who are not against such passionate hugs, then bruises are guaranteed.

Women who like to have sex for longer than five minutes, or couple of hours or perhaps one, two or three days, or even for a week, while taking only some shorts breaks, can get themselves an August 2nd born man with courage. He will be able to handle such a full, intimate and bright day or week. Of course, if an August 2nd born man is young and full of energy, then he will make an unforgettable impression on a woman. You can just use him or spend more time with him—whatever happens to be more convenient for you.

August 2nd's Dream Woman

If you are attracted to an August 2nd born man, it is only natural that you will need to act in order to get this man. You will need to present yourself in a way that an August 2nd born man's head will spin, and he will think that the woman you are playing is indeed his dream woman: a woman who makes him weak in the knees, who makes all his thoughts disappear.

Any woman who uses this recipe will have any August 2nd born man looking at her with devotion and puppy-like eyes. Before you decide to take him into your hands, find out who his parents are. If they are of strict moral rules, then you should definitely make a note of that. If he was some kind of a preacher, or some other type of philosopher who worked on self-development or enlightenment for a long period of time, then there may be some very interesting sexual additions depending on the philosophy that he studied. In other words, if someone wants to see a very sexy August 2nd born man with a hint of Christianity, such a sight will be unforgettable. An August 2nd born man with a Christian past will give such performance with pleasure.

Now, here is a recipe you can use to make this man yours completely in less than a five-minute conversation. First of all, a woman who wants to get an August 2nd born man must present herself as a woman with ambitions; she must show that she is energetic, sensual and ready to fight for this man against all other women who got their eyes on him as well. She must also show him that she is the number one among all these women who want to have him.

This woman does not like competitors and cannot stand when someone leaves her unnoticed, she would never allow that. She will use any methods in order to be first and will fight like a samurai. So, yes, do be scared ladies because you may find gum stuck in your hair, or something may accidentally get poured onto your dress, or your appearance may be totally ruined in some other way. You may also hear something so disturbing that you will not even want to complete against this other woman who wants to get this August 2nd anymore.

In addition, a woman should present herself as a successful woman, and if it is not like that in reality, then housework can also be considered work (because it is), and this woman can be very good at this job.

She must be very communicative and fearless, someone who does not care and is unstoppable, even by authorities. Bosses and leaders seem always very attractive to her because sex with them is another tool to use in order to move up in her career. So, even if you never experienced this, but you are trying to seduce an August 2nd born man, it is not difficult to make up a story like this actually happened. You can say that it was, for example, your current or ex-husband, or a former boyfriend, as long as at the moment that person is far away from the targeted August 2nd man.

In sex, this woman is not a sprinter, but rather a stayer. This woman should show the August 2nd born man right away that he has never met anyone like her, and that sex is not a five-minute process. She must be very interested in sex and enjoy variety. This woman must act like she is a professional as far as sex is concerned, and if in reality she is not, it is still possible to simply pretend and act like she is. At any rate, if she has doubts about her experience and sex techniques, then sex with any August 2nd born man will significantly broaden her horizons.

So, if you want to get an August 2nd born man, you must show that you do not ignore details in sex, and that everything interests you: where, how, at what time, for how long, etc. After all private details regarding the targeted August 2nd born man have been discussed, details like who he is, what he does, and how he got to this kind of life, the woman should focus on this man completely. She must show the August 2nd born man that no one else exists for her besides him, that she is absolutely swept away by him, totally charmed, and that she left all other thoughts behind. She must convince him that she is fully concentrated on his persona and that she wants him, wants to take him.

In other words, a woman should quite energetically show an August 2nd born man that he is her main goal. It is quite easy to show this. For example, keep staring at him, smile constantly, and do not forget to bend your body into some provocative positions.

A woman who is trying to seduce an August 2nd born man must look energetically joyful, as well as appear to be very creative in her proposals and ideas. Then, August 2nd will only need to choose which idea he prefers.

If after getting rid of her competitors, a woman sees an August 2nd born man and decides to take him by storm, it will be a very smart decision. Any August 2nd born guy will be completely charmed by this approach and will not be able to resist such a woman.

If the woman begins to happily chat about art, famous actors and singers and, at the same time, think of and share ideas about situations where it is possible to have sex, then no other woman will exist for an August 2nd born man besides her.

When you use this recipe, you should also mention or indicate that you are suffering. For example, a woman could say something like: "Oh, there is no man that would understand me, my creative side, my high energy and brave ideas that aim only at one thing: sunshine and happiness for everyone!" After this, a woman who is interested in an August 2nd born man should slowly, but surely move on and start dictating. Well, what does that mean? It means that you should start talking as if giving orders: "I want this and that. I want to see you again. I want you to stay, I want to go to a park, a casino, or some other place where it is noisy and exciting, where people are having fun." It can be a nice restaurant, but not a high-class one where all is quite, proper, but rather one where music is playing, where there are a lot of people, where everyone is enjoying themselves, where there is laughter, where one can get a drink or a few, where it is possible to tightly hug your partner while dancing, and to let your naughty hands feel who is who.

A woman who wants to seduce an August 2nd born man should also not be shy in her use of make-up, choice of hairdos, clothes, etc. Let your creative side shine through, try not to limit it; let your creativity come forward as fireworks and present yourself as a woman who is colorful like a peacock. This will make a huge impression on any August 2nd born man.

RECIPE 7

SECRET SEXUAL DESIRES OF WOMEN BORN ON AUGUST 11th OF COMMON YEARS (OR AUGUST 10th OF LEAP YEARS): RECIPE FOR SEDUCTION

If you want a woman born on August 11th, first of all, you should bewitch her with music of the rustling of bills of large denominations: under such an accompaniment, she will skillfully present you with "African passion!" To this woman, a man is just a "wallet on legs," one she can easily pay off with sex. Money and sex, why not?! "This man got an orgasm, I did too," - she argues, - "plus, I got money, so it is not at all bad, from any point of view."

To pay money in exchange for an orgasm is not unusual business; however, to get an orgasm for another's money is a skill. And, that is just the way an August 11th born woman acts. She can do many things: just do not attempt to force her to wake up early and strengthen her character by taking cold showers...

This woman is a legislator of all relations, but always for other people's money. Poor and miserable men do not interest her: she wants a man who is at the top, a leader, who always strives to be in the first row, to rise above all, one who does not hesitate to say things directly, openly, thinking that if one does not praise oneself—nobody else will! If she does find such a specimen then love, passion, with the full feedback of body and soul are possible for her, forgetting about everything, even about money... If you are capable of playing such Casanova, then this woman is yours.

It is easy to ensure that August 11th born woman accepts your invitation; simply tell her about the expected presence of rich, foreign visitors, a free-of-charge meat menu, exotic sweets, and expensive appetizers. This woman will not be able to refuse being present at such a free-of-charge event. By the way, she loves sweets very much. If you want to come into friendly contact, invite her to look at the dessert menu, and preferably after a good portion of meat.

Beware, though: if this lady gets back at you, her revenge will be merciless. In her revenge she will be persistent as a woodpecker, uncompromising as a bee.

You do not need to show off your sexual victory over her to your friends or fellow workers if she happens to works near you or at a competing company. She can create a great deal of trouble and will try to do everything to destroy your career.

Let's suppose you want to defeat her: you go and you threaten her. She will be frightened. It will be visible by the naked eye because she gets frightened very easily. You have calmed down. Great, it is done—you have threatened her, she got frightened and now she will be an obedient girl, you may think to yourself. The bad news is that she does not think that. She will act, and will calm down only when you get fired, for example, and with very bad recommendations. And, you will be absolutely sure that she had nothing to do with it.

If you promise an August 11th woman some personal property, real estate, career advancement, a trip to a sunny resort—she loves all this very much and for that can forgive you. If you cannot give that to her as compensation, then promise her all that to win time so you can change jobs or leave home as quickly as possible, otherwise she will begin to act.

If you are on good terms with an August 11th, she can become an excellent partner. It is easy to be friends with her. It is necessary to have a personality, to be a leader, have goals, and indomitably keep moving towards them; to have set career goals and to have financial success; to develop a high-tech product; etc. In other words, to strive for everything in life. Then, this woman will become an irreplaceable assistant, who will sell everything that you create, and will not allow you to be deceived and shortchanged.

August 11th's Anti-Dreams

If you are tired of an August 11th born woman, then do the following: simply turn into a constantly whining loser, captured by depression, unshaven, making a mess of the surrounding space, running somewhere in panic to rescue yourself. It is possible to accuse this woman of all failures, to tell her that it is she who has gotten you into a terrible, near suicidal condition, to accuse her of all sins and to make it melancholically, with a tear of hopelessness. This woman will then leave you alone, frightened herself as if she has actually done this to you. She will become depressed, will take antidepressants or get drunk, or might even shoot up drugs. It is not necessary to use this recipe. It is similar to putting some fiberglass into her favorite military-like slacks, only to be put on legs with highly sensitive skin. This woman has not deserved it, at least because she has shown you true passion and that does not happen often.

If you no longer want an August 11th born woman, it is enough to arrange a party for the nearest calendar holiday, or to suddenly arrange someone's unplanned birthday or presentation and invite this lady, stating that there will be rich foreign visitors, and unique foods and drinks will be had, and this lady will not be able to refuse. Your task: to feed her and get her drunk. Guests may or may not come, supposedly calling you and politely refusing. Having fed and, the main thing, having gotten her drunk, take her home. Then, carefully put her to bed, preferably in a warm room without drafts (she does not like cold and wind drafts), and wait until she falls asleep. Then, arrange her blanket in such a way that her lower back is exposed and open a window. Done—she will awake with either respiratory or kidney disease, and will have to deal with doctors for a long time. She will have no time for you or vendetta.

Only, please, do not overdo it—you and only you bear the full responsibility for her life since no one can ever prove your connection with her bad state of health. On the one hand, you are such a caring man. On the other hand, perhaps the situation is that this woman has decided to take a revenge on you, and you do not have a choice. It is certainly desirable to not lead a relationship with an August 11th to such an end...

RECIPE 8

SECRET SEXUAL DESIRES OF MEN BORN ON OCTOBER 13th OF COMMON YEARS (OR OCTOBER 12th OF LEAP YEARS): RECIPE FOR SEDUCTION

A man born on October 13th considers himself to be no more and no less than an earthly incarnation of god. He thinks of himself as the bearer of divine qualities and characteristics. Therefore, he claims to be god's representative on Earth, along with the status of the perfect ruler, king, emperor. He considers himself a generator of the only correct decision, and has the audacity to deny, permit, direct, supervise, manage, etc.

People born on October 13th always achieve everything they want. They idealize themselves a little, but who doesn't? If among your friends there are people born on October 13th and you wish to seduce them, below you will discover secrets about their sexuality.

In the sexual factor this man is very passionate: a constantly spewing, dynamic "volcano." He is a pronounced macho, a sort of super-male who displays typical male behavior, and typical male qualities: strength, courage, a desire to dominate, to compete, to win. In sexual relations, he is quite active and very fiery. With the ladies he loves to act big. He also is a great lover of brothels and is not against group sex...

An October 13th born man likes games very much. He enjoys all kinds of extreme situations, in life in general as well as in the sexual department.

During his resting time he likes to be left alone at home to engage in self-realization, go to brothels, enjoy magazines like the *Playboy*, etc.

Family for him is a welcomed part of life, a must-have. Family to him is holy, but that does not mean that it excludes all other affairs. For example, he pays special attention and has a special preference for married women.

This man can get extremely jealous. With his family, an October 13th born man can display himself as a typical tyrant and despot, although he can be very tender, especially with kids. He believes that children are all talented, and strives for his own to go to privileged schools. He loves his children from a distance, so to speak.

When making a decision about marriage, October 13th pays attention to the bride's wealth and could possibly get married for convenience. A grand wedding ceremony is a must for him.

The desire for luxury in this man is absolutely irresistible, especially when he is middle-aged. An October 13th born man wants to live in luxury; this is his need, and he must provide it for himself. Even if he was born into a poor family, it is not important, as he will strive for wealth anyway.

There is another interesting peculiarity: he recovers very quickly during a very short sleep. After twenty minutes of sleep, a completely exhausted, tired October 13th born man simply transforms. Therefore, keep in mind that if this man has been vehement in sex, presented you with a volcano (or rather was one) and you see that he is tired, do not worry—if he gets some sleep, twenty minutes later everything will start again. So, when he says that he is tired—he is not lying. He can nap for twenty minutes and recover fully.

It is possible to offer anal sex to October 13th, but not too much. This man enjoys very powerful sex, especially when the bed as well as the ceiling at the neighbor below shake. In the sexual factor, this person is convinced that he must be strong and powerful everywhere and always. What do women need to convince him of that? Passionate women who like powerful sex, sex that is strong, passionate and powerful enough to make the chandelier sway.

For this man, a period of romantic courtship is a must: the candy and flowers period is mandatory during courtship, and this period should be long and lush. He will be happy to do it because he enjoys it.

October 13th's Dream Woman

A woman who wants to seduce an October 13th born man must act as a queen, an empress, a limitless person. "I want this! I want that!" She does not understand, and does not take "No" for an answer; she has ambition and self-awareness as that of an empress. For her, there is only her and nothing else exists... It is important to play this role delicately, and not in a vulgar way. That is, to act like a true empress—with dignity. Keep in mind that any empress understands that no one will argue with her...

It is possible for a woman to take the initiative. In the case of an October 13th born man, it is appropriate for a woman to say "I want," but it must be done with a sense of dignity and royal majesty. She should let October 13th know what she wants, and that this is what she has decided. If she properly acts out an empress, the October 13th will submit to her on a subconscious level. He will even explain to himself why he did it.

An October 13th man likes when a woman enjoys romantic love-letters and serenades under her windows during the courtship period. In addition, she must love gifts, and in general, must love giving as well as receiving them (especially necklaces!).

A woman who wants to seduce an October 13th born man should also be jealous. In a situation where another woman is trying to seduce her man, for example, she must make a cardinal decision: "If I do not get him, no one gets him!"

October 13th's Anti-dreams

Do not be straightforward when communicating with an October 13th man, unless you want to see him run away from you. Also, do not hint at the possibility for you to have homosexual contacts.

Do not remind this man of the need to observe moral norms, although he himself can do it. In general, this person lives based on the following principle: "What is permitted to Jupiter is not permitted to a bull!" He can talk about moral values, and he sets them for other people, but not for himself.

Refrain from lecturing an October 13th born man, as this makes him terribly angry. Instead, if you want to activate him a bit more in bed, it will be good enough to pinch his buttocks... Just make sure to not lecture him.

If you want to keep an October 13th born man, avoid even hinting at the possibility of living separately while declaring that "family is a must." This person does not like that.

Also, keep in mind that when an October 13th man is in a bad mood, he becomes very unsociable.

RECIPE 9

SECRET SEXUAL DESIRES OF WOMEN BORN ON DECEMBER 7th OF COMMON YEARS: RECIPE FOR SEDUCTION

The essence of the sexual behavior of a woman who was born on December 7th can be expressed in the following: non-stop sex throughout life, or never ending sex. The women (and men too!) born on December 7th are simply obsessed with sex! For this woman it is not so important who she does it with, when she does it and where she does it—for her, sex is not an excuse to get acquainted.

What to do when the soul "calls for the sea" and she desires to, for example, be on board of a military tanker, where there are a lot of wild, beautiful, huge military guys?

Due to such interesting personal peculiarities, this woman very rarely "takes her head out of her underpants," so to speak. Without any hesitation, a December 7th born woman would order custom made underwear with a built-in vibrator. The idea behind this would be: put this underwear on, make sure the vibrator hits the right spot, turn it on and go out anywhere!

It is also completely possible for a December 7th woman to engage in various affairs, to work, to operate, to make orders, to command, to engage in business, politics, science... anything, because in fact, a December 7th born is not some thoughtless bagatelle—on the contrary, she is an extremely serious businesswoman.

In order to understand exactly how to seduce a December 7th born woman, it would be very convenient to know what she dreams about when it comes to sex. Let's take a closer look at some of December 7th born dreams and desires from her sexual factor.

Yes, You Are Right, Baby, I Am A Wild Man!

December 7th born women like all men in general, that is just their nature. However, there exists a certain type of males that a December 7th born simply cannot pass by calmly. They are the big, physically developed, muscular, tall and mighty body-builder type, men that cannot be fully embraced and reached. And, if they could be reached then for this woman it would be desirable to, right away, reach their "lower tie." However, in addition to all this, these men must be... fantastically ugly creatures: huge, ugly on the outside, short-haired *Frankensteins*!

If people born on any other day see a guy like this, only one idea will come into their head: "What a quasi-fashion!" Girlfriends of a December 7th born woman were surprised more than once by her preferences! For sure, many times they heard lies and vague explanations like "Appearance is not the main thing in men," followed by a list of male qualities: "soul, mind, character and other parameters." If instead she actually talked about "other parameters" that are way down between a man's legs—that would be much closer to the truth!

"So what if he is not an Alain Delon?" - thinks a woman born on December 7th - "It is dark at night anyway! And, it is always possible to cover a guy's face with a pillow!" Much more important is that he is an absolute male, like cowboys from American western movies, an experienced macho with a gun attached to his belt, with a whip in his hand, dressed in a shirt covered with sweat and dust from the road. Even if it is a biker who is dressed in leather and drinks something terrible on a regular basis, a man capable of winning a fight against anyone using his large fists, and of course the main thing... Well, you understand!

In other words, the man of a December 7th born woman's dreams is a rough unshaven dude who reeks of alcohol, smells of sweat and dirty socks, has a long beard between his legs, and who always misses the toilet bowl, as he does not at all burden himself with (from his point of view) unnecessary attempts to actually not miss it someday. Such a man will easily tear off December 7th's clothes. Then, he will twist her hair onto his hand, if the December 7th heroine has grown her hair out to be very long. Then, the man will inconsiderately bury December 7th's face in a pillow, and do it like there is no tomorrow! That is exactly what any December 7th born woman wants!

Basically, any partner, if he so desires, can create a sexual action under the name of "The Comeback of *Freddy Krueger*." A December 7th born woman will be delighted! For such a creative performance the following will be necessary: red contact lenses, red overalls or chain armour, weaved from round beads that remind of pearls or red caviar, and a red condom. Then, in the bedroom, in full darkness the man should somehow illuminate the room from below and jump out shouting wildly and with an open mouth. With his arms wide open, he should hold a piece of red rope with ends hanging down on each side. In order to fully complete this picture, it is also desirable to eat a clove of garlic. The smell will be terrible! "This is so terrifyingly wonderful!", a December 7th born woman would say.

An Office Romance

Work at a boring office in itself does not excite this loving December 7th Mademoiselle (by the way, if this woman does become a Madam, it will only be for a short while...). However, sex at a workplace is not just extremely attractive, but is an absolute must for a December 7th born woman! Otherwise, why go to work?

She will not leave a colleague, who is working hard and unattended on an urgent report at his desk, alone. She will take him by both ties: the top and the bottom! Phrases like "I am way too busy right now!" are capable of creating a burning fire of desire in a December 7th woman, and therefore leave no chance of stopping or preventing her solicitations.

The thought of gaining personal glory, a high social status, and money, in addition to everything else, is not so alien to this person, and she is ready to get it by any means necessary. This woman will come to the idea of connecting pleasant with useful sooner or later. Having sexual relations with "the necessary people," a December 7th born woman helps her career advancement and gets a release from sexual tension on a regular basis, and that is "just what the doctor prescribed!"

Industrial shops and factories where there are machines and conveyors, where there are busy men smeared in oil—those get special attention from a December 7th born woman. In such situations, she will always start bothering the object of her passion herself. This is how it happens: without being noticed she slips into the zone of reach of a working man at a moment when he is most busy (as that excites her very much), and starts to incline him towards sex. "Hello, John, the machine operator! Take off your trousers and let's get to know each other!" It does not matter that his overalls, face and hands have a thick layer of dirt, as a December 7th born woman will get all dirty with pleasure!

This woman is a big fan of obscene literary and vocal genres. Not only is she capable of remembering vulgar masterpieces by heart, but she is also able to compose them herself by, for example, altering poems of classics. A December 7th born woman loves dirty jokes, especially ones that have, for example, lieutenants as one of the characters. Here is an example of an anecdote that December 7th would enjoy:

"While searching for his girlfriend in a large house with many rooms, the lieutenant had intimate relations with everyone whom he came across during his search. Then, at last, he saw his girlfriend and with his voice filled with anguish said: "Oh, darling! I had such a hard time while looking for you!" Sounds awfully vulgar? Well, yes! And, this is exactly what any December 7th born woman likes! Here is another example: "... And then came the libertine and said: "We shall take a little walk, Pinocchio!" A December 7th woman would definitely appreciate and enjoy this joke as well.

She also likes lieutenants as owners of huge sexual experience and ones who are always ready. "You are a sex maniac!" – a December 7th woman would tell him, only to add – "Seems I did not make a mistake by choosing you!" Oh, how she loves sex maniacs! In fact, this is what she is herself: a sex maniac.

There is a fine joke on this account (Yes, an awfully vulgar one, which is exactly what excites both women and men who were born on December 7th): "A *Little Red Riding Hood* is walking through dark woods alone, as always. Suddenly a reporter jumps out of the bushes and asks: "Pardon me, but aren't you afraid of walking alone in the woods? You know, anything can happen in the woods, like rape, for example?" The *Little Red Riding Hood* answers: "Well, the reason I walk alone in the woods is because I love having sex!" That is how December 7th born are: *Little Red Riding Hoods* throughout their lives.

A word of caution for the "wolves": those men who decide to have sex with December 7th woman should be very cautious, as first of all, it is questionable who will "rape" whom in the end. Secondly, after doing it with a December 7th born woman, some may barely survive!

If a December 7th born woman lives in some residence hall, a sex-tour with the neighbors is guaranteed! She would not miss anyone, and would engage in sex on a regular basis, visiting one floor after another. She considers herself to be a respectable woman, and it really is true because a December 7th born woman does everything (and everyone) in order!

She also enjoys going to doctors, as she is not against seducing some *Aesculapius* (see Roman mythology) directly in his office! And, if she herself becomes a doctor, and that is quite possible, then she will regularly combine business with pleasure, connecting traditional methods of treatment of patients with not so traditional ones that, from her point of view, are useful for their health.

In fact, sex is the best medicine, isn't that true? It is unimportant if it is or not for others, but for a December 7th born woman that statement certainly is true. Sick people are usually prescribed a few days of bed-rest by doctors. "Why roll around the bed without doing anything?" thinks a December 7th. This woman does not like idleness.

There is a fine joke about doctors who are similar to people born on December 7th: a female client comes to see a male psychologist. As soon as she enters his office, he jumps on her and takes her without a word. Having finished his business, he buttons his trousers and says: "Well, I have already solved my problem. So, what was the problem that you came here with today?"

Tender Murderer: Soft Masochism & Hard Sadism

This woman is very tactile. Long massages raise her desire, and she will not refuse to massage her partner as well. Since she has an unrestrained desire to bite, and experiences original sensations like an "itch" of her own teeth, the massage that she gives her partner can look like systematic biting of all of his body. She will not refuse the idea of being prodded with sharp objects. At the moment of strong excitement, when the pain threshold becomes high enough, in order to strengthen her sexual sensations, the sex organ of her partner can be placed in a special condom with sharp spikes covering the surface. This will work especially well when the partner is behind her, and the prickly surface comes in contact with her buttocks.

Also, she might enjoy the use of nails or sharp objects around her neck, head, back and thighs, but without damage to the skin. Be careful to poke, but not to scratch because scratches can end very badly... for her partner that is! It is best not to joke with this woman. Painful pressure against her skin during sexual contacts always occurs, as it is directly connected with the increase of the pain threshold during arousal. However, for this woman, any damage to her skin is absolutely unacceptable. If that happens, she will go wild with the skin of her partner.

A similar tactic of causing pain can occur in the following way: first, easy, pleasant, tactile touches (from her side that is), then active, stronger squeezes of her partner's body and neck, including choking her partner at the moment of orgasm. The algorithm of reaching orgasm, together with pain, can become constant and indispensable for this woman. In some cases it can get to extreme forms, and may include heavy damage of her partner's body or even worse. However, it all depends on the degree of her attachment to the described algorithm.

Here Everyone Kisses Under Every Bush

A December 7th woman likes sexual experiments, including oral sex in the most unusual places. For example: on thick grass, at enclosed silent places (a tent, a stack of hay, an attic, a cellar), directly in the river, on a riverboat, on an airplane, at various public places (a movie theater, a fitting room, a beach, etc.). For her, there is only one rule: engage in sex everywhere! For this woman's sexual joy, there are places that are extremely attractive, like sheds and tents. However, the best entertainment for her are trips to natural parks, planned and organized in a manner of an army gathering, with camp, bonfires, precise military schedule and with a sergeant (or better, several sergeants) in a military uniform.

The following situations are madly attractive to her: sex in space limited by a circle of burning fire, where it becomes possible to feel the heat of the fire, and smell burnt hair; sex in a tent on rough linens, and slaps of a soldier's belt on buttocks; sex in the woods, among bushes with thorns, for example. When going on such camping trip, it is not a bad idea to take some camouflage paint or take advantage of black soot from the fire, and put it on the face and body of the man. This will seriously strengthen the passion of the December 7th woman.

I Love The Military. They Are So Beautiful And Huge!

One more way of entertainment for this woman is to rest and have a good time, while pretending to be someone else, and it is not important whom. The idea behind this is simple: having planned out the route in advance (and the destination can be, for example, the next town over, or any city where no one knows her), she puts on clothes according to the chosen strategy. There, she will meet a man and tell him a story that is completely imaginary from beginning to end. She will use all kinds of fables since the imagination of this woman as well as her eloquence depend not only on her cultural-educational level, but also on her degree of desire to do it with yet another man.

As mentioned above, women born on December 7th are very much attracted to military guys. Therefore, the object of sexual travel can quite possibly be a military base or any military school. Once in the barracks, this woman will not waste any time. Without waiting for the hungry and mad with happiness soldier to undress, she will unbutton his uniform belt and will take hold of a man's main advantage. This woman loves and is very skilled at oral sex! As far as cap and boots, a December 7th born woman thinks that it is not necessary to remove them, especially since she finds it pleasant when man's feet stink. In the process of copulation this woman will absolutely let the whole area know about it with loud moans and shouts. She will count on thin walls, and the fact that soon doors from adjacent rooms will start to open up, and the hallway will fill up with noise from the boots of officers wanting to join in on the action. Why not? Group sex is just what she wants! An ability to have multiple orgasms is one of physiological qualities of this woman. However, after having multiple sets of orgasms, and therefore satisfying her sexual appetite a little bit, a December 7th born woman will very quickly disappear—the business is now finished.

December 7th born women think that they are the greatest teachers of all times. This woman likes to teach and is especially dangerous to young, cute and shy men who have never been kissed below the belt before. Without thinking twice, this woman will "teach them how to love life!" December 7th born people will never turn down a request to help loose virginity. Naturally, any December 7th born person (man or woman) will surely sleep with the pupils and students of the institution where she happens to teach. And, have no doubt, it is very easy to pass an exam with this person in exchange for "it."

This woman likes not only to tempt, but also to be tempted or seduced, and preferably in a dirty way. For her it is necessary to constantly justify her promiscuity to herself and to others. Therefore, she chooses a convenient position called "a victim of circumstances." She will say: "They seduced me in a perverted and artistic manner," but she will not explain why it happened specifically to her and what she did in order for it to happen. "These men that only want one thing have involved me in sexual relations, and I had to do it for the sake of... business!" she will say. However, the most amusing thing is that with time she forgets that, using the language of December 7th born people, "this was a cheap excuse for idiots" and begins to believe it herself!

Moreover, it becomes an interesting sexual game when she is "forced" to have sex or is being seduced like an innocent, pure girl, as she has many fantasies on this topic. They can be materialized in various role-play games, like the teacher seducing a student; torture chambers and officers of *Gestapo*; boss engaging in sex with his secretary; a mean doctor who uses the weaknesses of his patients; an artist-maniac, who, instead of engaging in art, draws on canvas using not at all a brush, and takes advantage of naked and "defenseless" December 7th...

The main and most important thing is that she had nothing to do with any of it! She makes sure that in the end it will be possible to make a helpless gesture and say: "It just happened!" or "All men are such swines and seducers!" And, of course, she will not mention anything about what she did to provoke the given situation.

Porn Stars Rest When December 7th Takes Business Into Her Hands

A December 7th born woman is not at all against posing a bit. But, certainly, it is better not to just pose! She wants to be naked in front of a photographer with a very large... lens! She likes, to put it mildly, nude style photos of herself, and together with them shameless porn films, where she plays the leading roles. In general, any opportunity to engage in sex when there is an audience present, risking to get both prolonged applause and "Bravos!" is attractive to her.

If there is no opportunity to become a porn star, December 7th will do everything on a regular basis to cause erection in any man that she encounters. And, it is unimportant whether or not she is interested in him as a sexual partner. The main thing is for his fly to crack as soon as he sees her, resulting in a "concussion" from his member banging on his forehead! In order to achieve this goal, special behavior and different means of improvisation are used: skirts more resembling a belt, cleavage all the way down to her shoes, wet sexual lips half the size of her face, etc.

As has already been mentioned in parallel with the *Little Red Riding Hood* anecdote, a December 7th born woman can be considered a sex terrorist. If for any reason she is unable to "communicate" with the object of her desire, she can then easily commit a crime on sexual grounds, so to speak. "Many men are much better than not enough men! I will find use for them!"

Participation in various orgies is incredibly attractive to her, especially when many men participate as well. However, there is one important condition: there must not be any women! Actually, it is simply way too hazardous to the health of any female participants.

A Cannibal Does Not Lecture, But Simply Eats!

Imagine an oval-shaped bedroom, almost like the *Oval Office* in Washington D.C. (USA), but more resembling an operational room at a hospital: light walls, white ceiling, white blinds, a bare minimum of furniture... In other words, only that, what is most necessary. In the center of a room, instead of a bed there is an operational table in a form of a cross. Above the table there are powerful lights that also generate heat. A December 7th woman makes a man lie down on the table, then tightly secures his arms, legs and head using belts to make sure that he does not escape. Now the man is entirely and completely doomed! This sacrificial body is tormented on the table, while being heated by the infernal lights from above. Now all that remains is to simply add some garnish and start having it part by part...

Scary as it may sound, this is what women born on December 7th like! There is actually an amusing anecdote that wonderfully illustrates this topic. A man asks a woman to give him a blow job. In turn, she asks to put some jam on his organ so that it becomes tastier, then adds some peanuts, some sugar, and some crumbled up cookies. When she is ready for the process itself, she hears the following from her man: "It looks so good! I will eat this myself!" This could be an amusing joke, but... not with a December 7th born woman!

The following may be used to serve the "table": cut fruit, whipped cream, which can be applied in the form of patterns over the body of the partner, or some hot dense syrup to burn his skin with. All this magnificence will be consumed by a December 7th before and during the sexual act. She will bite various places of her partner's body, and in order to not bite off something important during moments of passion, she will continue to eat fruit (Although she certainly loves to eat meat much more, but that would be a criminal offense!). A December 7th woman can freely approach this buffet in the center of a bedroom many times from any side, taking pleasure from strong chained parts of the man's body one by one—arms, legs, head and, certainly, his penis! In fact, the main thing for her is to have multiple orgasms. Having climbed up on the table, she will saddle the soiled lover, and will rush off towards wild orgasms! And, while galloping, she will most definitely put a handful of orange pieces into the mouth of the man, so that he begins to choke and shake, trying to clear his throat. Similar spasms and convulsions of the partner strongly raise a December 7th born woman's desire.

When she becomes weak after dinner and rough sex, she is capable of falling asleep directly on her partner's body. However, this woman does not like messy rooms or dirt neither on herself nor others. Therefore, after events like the one described above, without fail both them (if the partner managed to stay conscious and healthy) and the bedroom will get carefully cleaned and washed.

"Vegetables are not only tasty, but also... well, useful for staying healthy!" that is what this woman believes. She also combines food and sex in the following way: during periods of asceticism (which happen regularly in her life, as she is not a supporter of residing jointly with a man) she wants sex just as much. Therefore, besides a vibrator, she uses products from the vegetable store: carrots, cucumbers, zucchini, etc.

Besides dreams there are of course anti-dreams, and it is equally important to know them as well. Below are some things that all women born on December 7th do not like.

December 7th's Anti-Dreams

Of course, there are situations, people and things that are capable of depriving of sexual inclinations even such a sex terrorist as a December 7th! For example, bugs are intolerable by this woman. She would never engage in sex on a bed with bugs, ants, fleas or anything like that! Any hint of these, or a joke with spreading beans all over a bed-sheet, or an offer to glance under a blanket to see what "big bug" got under there, will make a December 7th literally take off immediately. Upon understanding that it was a joke, she will tastefully send the joker to hell, using multiple unpleasant expressions.

She also does not like any kind of female advances, even friendly ones! And, she certainly does not like sex with the participation of other women. However, it may be that she will give it a try once in her life! The only thing is that, as mentioned above, such experiments are very dangerous for her female partner.

Also, December 7th born women hate beds... anything one can lie down on: cots, mattresses, rugs, as well as lace linens, pink coverlets and decorative small pillows. She hates all that. She also dislikes anything hanging above the bed, like canopies, as well as handrails or poles near the bed. In other words, both women and beds cause attacks of debauch in December 7th.

In addition, a December 7th can easily be pushed away by men who look like dwarves, and men who are simply short, especially if they have the habit of wearing hats, or, even worse, those silently releasing gas, spoiling the air around them with a mean smell.

A man who, due to his imprudence, decides to decorate the body of a December 7th with meat or fish products, wishing to eat them off of her as if from a table, will receive a slap on his face without any further discussion.

An owner of a bright and colorful tie, who takes a chance and introduces himself to a December 7th born woman, will be sent away with anger. The same will happen to "fruitcakes" in swimming trunks of similar colors, for example, if this occurs at a beach where she prefers to spend her summer holidays. However, the most disgusting, shocking, gross men for a

December 7th born woman are homosexuals! If she had the power and free time, she would destroy all of them in the whole Universe in a gas chamber of her own private residence. But first, she would castrate them. Therefore, any hint of femininity in a man, excessive gallantry, elegance or manners will pose only one question for a December 7th born woman: "Well, well, where are my garden scissors!?"

For whom else cry the nut-cutting scissors? Another example would be a collector of refined objects, who appreciates matrimony, fidelity and monogamy; a man who has reached his goals, for example a professional who is well off; a silent leader; a man who is quiet, safe, stable, idle with a peaceful lifestyle; a man who after coming home from work every day sits in the coziness of a soft armchair in the company of his Persian or Angora cat; a man who has plants by his windows; one who holds deep conversations about humanity, mercy and love for people—his sexual behavior will be silent and quiet, with smooth slow frictions. "We will do it slowly and sadly..." such a man may say. December 7th born women hate that!

A type of men that she hates will even undress a woman in an original way: he will draw her skirt upwards and will lower her blouse downwards in such a way that her clothes would still remain on her and will be dangling around her waist. Having drunk one or two glasses of brandy, for example, such a man will fall asleep directly on his partner during the process of sex. This man also loves visitors, especially relatives, and participates in their destiny with sensitivity. For example: he dresses them, slowly feeds them, gives them drinks, holds heart-to-heart talks and by doing so tries to help these misled people find their place in society, he gives recommendations, and helps contact the necessary people. "Hold on a moment!" a December 7th born woman would say: "Where are we going to have sex if the house is full of relatives and orphans?!" She will send such a man to the same place where she sent the owners of bright swimming trunks and homosexuals.

In addition to the fact that the sexual intemperance of this woman forces her to run to orthodox temples and monasteries on a regular basis, she is simply drawn to debauchery. A man who believes in god with obligatory Sunday church attendance, who leads an ascetic, almost angelic life, who is comfortable, stable and predictable, will have a negative contact with any December 7th born woman.

RECIPE 10

SECRET SEXUAL DESIRES OF MEN BORN ON DECEMBER 21st OF COMMON YEARS: RECIPE FOR SEDUCTION

Ladies, if you are bored and feel like you have experienced and tried it all, visited all the possible places and saw everything, or if you are just feeling blue; maybe you just want to try something not new, but original; if you are brave enough, or even better, if you are curious... Then, do yourself a favor and find a man who was born on December 21st. You will not regret it, but do be careful!

A man who was born on this date is the true Demon of the Night! A demon, who haunts for women's hearts, passion, love, and their luscious bodies. He strives for each rendezvous to become an unforgettable experience... at least for him. If you do some research, you will definitely find such a man not too far from where you live. Obviously, beauty is in the eye of the beholder... Hopefully, you will find an attractive example, but the most important thing is that he is a December 21st born!

In order to entertain yourself (sexual entertainment, that is since we are talking about the sexual factor of this man) you do not need to go to some exotic place like Amsterdam, Thailand or Brazil. Oh no! Just the mere presence of this magnificent man with incredible self-control is enough, and the only reason he masters this self-control is to charm, fascinate and seduce. This is his natural gift. There are some men who possess multiple talents. However, in this case, this man not only has the talent to allure, but also, the sexual talent to leave the impression of a partner who can always be there for you! All you have to do is just offer yourself to this man, offer him a chance to conquer you, offer him an opportunity to seduce you. Of course, you could also resist him a little to heat things up.

If you merely know each other, he may begin telling you about his strong ethical values. If he is married, for example, he will tell you that he has been married for a long time and his marriage is strong, but suddenly, you will notice that this conservative man is expressing some peculiar interest in you, as if he were getting ready to indulge in the act of seduction. If this happens, you are so lucky! This man loves starting affairs according to all the romance rules. Beautiful courtship is guaranteed! However, keep in mind not to get carried away, and protect yourself from getting in the long list of already seduced and utilizable women. Yet, if you like that, keep in mind that you will have a certain number assigned to you in the aforementioned list, and this list is not short!

If you allow this man to charm you, then be prepared to witness a very extravagant, eccentric, creative, and even somewhat crazy show. You can compare it to the theatrical performance of a sex-actor, who creates a show just for you. Soon, in a more intimate setting, you will experience all of the incredible tricks, which he has created specifically for you! This is a man who knows how to find the right key to any woman, but be warned: do not lose your head.

December 21st born man surely knows how to kiss. Women love good kissers, but his kiss is something mystical, something beyond your wildest dreams, something out of this world. Even so, this man will sometimes overdo it.

His theatrical performance depends on how young he is, though he has more than enough strength. And, be prepared—after your intimate encounter, you will be unwinding yourself for a long time from the position in which he left you. It is possible that after an intimate meeting with a December 21st man you will resemble a spectacular flat picture like on an advertising board, for this man is capable of imprinting you in the sheets. So keep that in mind as well!

If you have enough courage and strength to withstand this man, then you found a worthy partner who will compete with you until the last breath: he loves it! In this case, keep in mind that competing with him will not be an easy task for you because the more you compete, the more strength he has. Also, know that after these competitions, he desires to do something extraordinary, non-traditional, something unusual even more since his sexual tool kit is unlimited. And, he does everything in his power to try his entire kit, at the same time fully knowing how to use his main tool.

Ladies, you do not have to go to Rio to have a sensational carnival, you can find it in any December 21st born man: he will surely perform well in bed, or on any surface for that matter, and his performance will be designed specifically for you! A December 21st born man is quite a catch! If you are attracted to him, you may want to know what his dream woman is like and how to behave around this magnificent man. Below is a recipe to attract this man and use him in all respects as intended.

December 21st's Dream Woman

First of all, a woman of his dreams is stylish. Everyone has a different sense of style, but here it has to be simple, yet chic. Imagine a beautiful, well-formed, and slick fountain pen with a cap, framed with small and tasteful diamonds, a golden nib and quality engraving. Now apply this example to her appearance: this woman wears skin-tight and very stylish clothes. She behaves around a December 21st born man as if she finally found her beloved "daddy," one who is capable of everything, knows everything, and is willing to do anything for his favorite girl. This woman tells a December 21st man that her dream has finally come true and that with him she feels happy. She behaves as if everybody around her is envious that she is with this incredible man! It does not matter if it is a corporate event or a party for friends—she shows December 21st that only with him she feels like a woman! You know how to do this, dear women!

If you chose to hunt down a December 21st man you should not present yourself to him in the following way unless you want to get rid of him: he despises a woman who is self-sufficient, ambitious and behaves as if she is royalty, a woman who bosses around and commands, constantly demands others to serve her needs—"Bring that!", "Get out!", etc. Such commands will not work with December 21st.

When a woman meets a December 21st man, she says that she welcomes those men, whose goal is to have a good family, durable house... or, to be honest, an expensive house; those men who care about their family, their wife, their parents. She mentions in the conversation with him that she wants stable, normal, civilized family relations, where equality and democracy rule, where partners consult with each other, and where a man is respected and awaited! She makes it clear that a man holds the key to a healthy relationship between a man and a woman.

Also, do not forget to say something like "Dear December 21st, I can be a jealous woman! I am very jealous and revengeful! If I notice that there is anything wrong with your behavior, if something causes me to think that you pay attention to other women, you better think twice!" This woman is very cruel when she is angry, and her vengeance has no limits if December 21st starts fooling around.

Hint to this Demon of the Night that it would be a good idea to continue your encounter somewhere by the ocean, at the beach, lie in the sand with or without umbrellas, where there are palm trees and sun since this woman feels great in such environment. Only in these warm conditions she can exist with no worries, and if such a great man accompanies her, then it is just perfect! Then, the intimate relations will be very impressive and alluring.

Also, she should be very clear: no matter how virginal she acts, or if she claims to be oriented around building a good family, she is not a prude! She welcomes sex in any form… oral, usual, unusual… she is up for anything.

Despite being fragile, this woman is very strong: she can twine around him with such strength that he feels that she becomes a sexual continuation of him, as if he merged with his beloved second half since his half finally has been found. Women can take advantage of this and give December 21st these exact sensations by making it clear to him that he found his other half in you. He is very interested in his dream to find his "other half." Use this recipe on any December 21st man, apply it and you will see that that is exactly how it is.

Also, this woman loves embracing, hugging and cuddling. She embraces with passion and her hugs are firm, so the December 21st man should be cautious that this woman does not choke him in her passion…

Ladies, you have to love oral sex when you are with a December 21st man. When it comes to oral sex, he will just watch a woman to make sure she does not bite something off! However, if she does not bite it off, she can chew it at least a little bit because this man likes that a lot.

When it comes to regular and anal sex, all surfaces should be suitable for her. And, if you combine oral and anal sex together, this man will never forget the experience. For more details on how to combine oral, anal, and regular sex you can read other literature, of which there is plenty online. If you want to win over a December 21st man, you can look at some pictures if you do not know anything about this, although it is doubtful that you do not…

In between intercourse, this man needs a massage. He loves when someone scratches his back, massages around his neck, and in order to make this man spark, such stimulating massage can come in handy. He will be back to life very soon and can "attack" you again.

If this man is still in good health he does not get easily tired in bed. If you cannot handle his pace, when enough is enough, just turn on the air conditioner, so that the room is fully vented and chilly. This is simply a recommendation on how to cool things down with him, so you can get some rest as he will get the urge to leave you alone for a little while.

Also, do not forget to mention to December 21st that if the relationship with him continues, you will find a lot of ways to make him warm, will cuddle him all the time and will be there for him during difficult times. Let this magnificent man hear from you that not only you found your dream in him, but you are also ready to sacrifice everything just to give him a hug and warm him up in your arms.

If for some reason the above recipe is too difficult for you to perform, then try simply mimicking this December 21st man, adapt his behavior and copy him. Obviously be creative with it, show some talent, interpret his representation from the female perspective and mirror his behavior back to him. He will not remain indifferent to such a woman!

EPILOGUE

I would like to end this book with a quote:

"It is meaningless to stand by ideas of naturalism, harmonious life, unity with Nature, and organics if your life is anti-Nature, because a tiger chewing on millet is a mutant, and Nature is known to destroy all mutants, individually and collectively. Our civilization is built on anti-Nature principles; a civilization that has no basis in the form of the *Catalog of Human Population (Catalog Of Human Souls)* will sooner or later be destroyed. We are still alive because humanity is very small compared to Nature, so we cannot inflict serious and irreparable harm to Nature. Nature can exist without humanity; humanity cannot exist without Nature. Maybe it makes sense to try to be as close to Nature as possible.

And, for those who do not want to continue to use stupid advice or recommendations that are harmful to their health, can now request information from the most ancient sources of knowledge, the *Shan Hai Jing*. There are many problems in people's lives, but the solution to all of them is in a single place. To make one's life a real life, to make it truly interesting, bright, positive, effective (and truly Natural!), one must know the answer to just one question–"Who am I?" Once you know who you are, it becomes clear what to do or not to do, how to behave, how to live. Knowing your program is the way to true organics–the organic matter of your soul." *Olga Skorbatyuk*

APPENDIX

ABOUT THE *CATALOG OF HUMAN POPULATION* (CATALOG OF HUMAN SOULS)

The source of research materials presented is the ancient Chinese manuscript called *Shan Hai Jing*, a manuscript that is well-known among sinologists. In 1975, a scientific Laboratory founded by Andrey Davydov and Olga Skorbatyuk made a breakthrough discovery: it was found that this manuscript is not a mysterious description of flora, fauna and chimeras of the mythical world, but instead, it contains coded descriptions of about 300 unique human subtype structures or human programs. They are recorded in *Shan Hai Jing* by images.

What does this mean? Well, to understand this let's use an analogy: consider animals, for example; animal is the type, while elephants, deer, tigers, etc. can be considered subtypes. Elephants and tigers are both animals, however, (and you will surely agree) a tiger is not an elephant, and they differ from each other and from other animals, significantly. So, it is clear that every animal subtype has its own unique psycho-physiological structure and characteristics, or subtype program implanted by Nature. Scientists discovered that this is similar with *Homo sapiens*! In other words, humans also have subtypes, and every subtype has its own unique psycho-physiological structure or subtype program.

With further research, scientists found a method that allowed them to identify which subtype any given person belongs to and, therefore, how all humanity is classified. Human subtypes are based on phenological cycles and are identified using the date of birth. Why? Because each type of living organism comes to the world at times strictly allocated to it.

Rabbits, for example, give birth at the end of April-beginning of May; deer in May-June; seals in March-April; and this is similar with humans. For example, all people born on March 5th of common years (or March 4th of leap years) have the same psycho-physiological structure or subtype program. This means that, considering the current world population of about 7.1 billion, every human program describes approximately 20 million people born on the same day.

Scientists developed the technology further and were able to decrypt (decode) or, in other words, read and translate, every human program and laws of human Nature described in the *Shan Hai Jing* manuscript. This technology is a result of systematic research in the field of psycho-physiology, and enables scientists to fully identify the psycho-physiological structure or program of any person.

In 2005, using this new technology, researchers proved that the *Shan Hai Jing* manuscript is the source of knowledge of human Nature. Scientists continued to decode the source, and began to compile their main intellectual product: the *Catalog of Human Population (Catalog of Human Souls)*. It includes about 300 unique human subtype programs and three manipulation modes (suppression, balance, stimulation) for each program.

It is important to note that knowledge of information from the Catalog about yourself and how you can be manipulated makes you immune to manipulation by others, and releases you from all kinds of "guilt trips" and similar discomforts that eventually end in psychological distress. In addition, with this knowledge your happiness will no longer depend on anyone but you. Moreover, every person is capable of stabilizing and restoring the health of their own psyche by themselves, without the need of social workers, religious figures or other organizations: it is all possible with the knowledge of your individual subtype program and manipulation modes.

With the Catalog you can have power in any amounts that you want, have an exciting life and great health regardless of age, have so much money you could swim in it, experience continuous enjoyment instead of constant boredom and "misfortune," etc.! Real estate, stones and gold do not matter—the best investment is always in your own self, regardless of what it is you are investing: time, money, intellect, etc. Always invest in yourself: that is the only proven way to get what you want and as much of it as you want.

WHAT IS THE CATALOG OF HUMAN POPULATION AND WHAT IS HUMAN PSYCHE?

1. Scientific psychology and researcher's, author of scientific discovery Andrey Davydov's finding of the answer to the question "What is human psyche and what is its structure?" in one of the most ancient monuments preserved in our civilization.

People of this civilization have long been convinced that each one of them is unknowable. This is not surprising since it is much easier for "the powerful ones" to control ignorant masses in order to use them. However, Homo sapiens was created in such a way that he does not stop being interested in what he is, and how his psychophysiology1—the sum of psyche and body—is arranged, despite that this interest could not find satisfaction for many centuries. Religion offered quite an amusing, to put it mildly, vision of these issues, and psychology, until recently, was unable to provide authentic information to the most elementary questions of an individual, such as "Who am I?" and "What am I?" For none of the existing methods, which psychologists have, despite their variety, allowed to look inside the human soul.

Although psychologists tried to find a way out of this situation, from our point of view—these attempts were quite unsuccessful. Contrary to that words 'soul' and 'psyche' are synonymous (from the Ancient Greek ψυχικός "soul, soulful," from ψυχή—"soul"), representatives of scientific psychology separated them without much hesitation. Soul was taken out of the scope of their studies, declared a phantom and left to religion, while under the label "psyche" they began to study anything at all: "phenomena of consciousness", "direct experience of the subject," his behavior, intellect, etc. It got to that intellect was practically announced to be the soul. That is, psychologists are not even aware of that intellect is not psyche, but only a part of psyche. Moreover, it is a secondary part (more on this will be presented below).

All in all, it turns out that the science of psychology was never a science because it never had and does not have any idea about the subject of its study—the soul, psyche. Moreover, it persistently ignores its subject, even though "psychology" translated from the Ancient Greek means "science of the soul" (from the Ancient Greek ψυχή—"soul"; λόγος—"teaching"). Scientific status of psychology not only became the topic of extensive debates, but also is denied by psychologists themselves. As noted by A. V. Yurevich (the deputy director of the Institute of Psychology of Russian Academy of Sciences) in 2005, psychology occupies an intermediate position between science and pseudoscience. And, surprisingly, psychologists are fine with this.

However, despite everything, at the end of the XX century answers to questions "What is human psyche and what is its structure?" and many others—were found. To put it simply: the human soul was opened liked a tin can. Scientists decrypted one of the most ancient monuments preserved in this civilization, and it turned out that this source contains a detailed description of the structure and mechanisms of work of human psyche. (Or human soul, whatever you prefer.)

The name of this ancient monument is 山海經 (Shānhǎi Jīng, Shan Hai Jing, translated as the Catalog of Mountains and Seas, Book of Mountains and Seas). Precise dating of this monument is still not available, but some researchers date it XXIII century BC. In the 70s of the XX century, that is—almost forty centuries after the presumptive appearance of the above-mentioned monument in this civilization, sinologist and researcher of ancient books Andrey Davydov posed a question: "What is the Catalog of Mountains and Seas? Is it an unclear treatise or the richest collection of images, which are directly related to a human and his psyche?" This question was not empty because images of strange beings, often of chimerical nature, remained in practically all cultures of the world, but nowhere, except for in the Catalog of Mountains and Seas, these images were systematized into something whole that could be called a catalog. And, Andrey Davydov found the answer to this question. Shan Hai Jing indeed turned out to be a map of psychophysiological structure of Homo sapiens—the Catalog of human population.

This ancient source was qualified as the Catalog of the human population on the basis of the fact that Andrey Davydov found in it detailed descriptions of 293 archetypal structures of human psyche. This clearly indicated that the biological type "human" is divided into subtypes (subspecies), and Shan Hai Jing describes the psychophysiological arrangement of each one of them, similar to catalogs, encyclopedias about animals, anatomical atlases, etc.

In the course of many years (from 1975 to 1995) of research, Andrey Davydov not only managed to create a unique technology for decryption of Shan Hai Jing, but also decrypted the information found in this source. This information included description of the arrangement and work of psychophysiology of 293 human subtypes, as well as details about the natural toolkit for managing a human in the form of descriptions of natural manipulation modes for each subtype, and a lot of other interesting information related to natural arrangement of Homo sapiens.

It became clear that the opinion (which is still widespread) that at the moment of birth a human is "a tabula rasa" ("a blank slate"), on which anyone, including himself, could write anything that he pleases, like on a blank sheet of paper, is a fallacy. Detailed descriptions of 293 structures of human psyche, which were discovered in the ancient monument, clearly demonstrated that every person is born with a natural program, in which everything is implanted: what he will be like, how he will live, down to the smallest details. It turned out that the soul does exist. And, it is not some kind of unknowable value or a phantom. Using the computer terms, the soul (psyche) is the "software" of Homo sapiens.

One's own soul or the soul of another is no longer a mystery because from descriptions, which were discovered in Shan Hai Jing, it is possible to obtain any kind of information about any one of over 7,000,000,000 representatives of the biological type Homo sapiens living on this planet. However, it is not a mystery only to those, who have access to decrypted information from this ancient source. The rest still have to ask psychologists and society: "Who am I? What am I?" and receive absurdity and someone's imagination in response.

In parallel, psychology got a chance to be called science. After all, owing to many years of research work carried out by Andrey Davydov, answers to questions "What is the soul (psyche) of a human and what is its structure?" were found. They were discovered in the Catalog of human population, which turned out to be ancient writings, heritage of our ancestors or maybe our creators because the authorship of this source is undetermined. Decryption of Shan Hai Jing, as translation from the language of ancient images into the language of modern descriptions of life and functioning of two hundred and ninety three human subtypes, formed the basis for the Non-traditional Psychoanalysis, as a new direction in scientific psychology. This direction factually made it a science.

However, something else is more important. With the return of the Catalog of human population to this civilization, every person living on earth (and their descendants) has a chance to become a human. Currently, there is not a single human (according to the meaning of this word, which is recorded in the catalog that describes humanity) present on this planet. Ancient writings clearly state that one is not born a human, but one can become a human with the help of a certain, specific method—learning; learning as studying and mastering one's own natural "software." Moreover, this includes going through multiple levels of development. However, it is not possible to become a human without the "textbook" called the Catalog of Mountains and Seas.

1 We use the term "psychophysiology" because for us the issue, which is still being discussed by psychologists—"What is primary: psyche or physiology?"—has long been settled. We know that psyche is primary. However, having no relation to religion, we do not separate the body and the soul, and we do not consider the soul as something that exists by itself, apart from the body. And, in fact, this is not our personal opinion—this also is information from ancient texts, which appeared long before Torah, Bible, and so on.

2. What is the soul (psyche) of a human and what is the Catalog of human population?

Soul (psyche) of a human is an archetypal matrix. Or, if we draw an analogy with a computer, "a hard disk," on which natural "software" of Homo sapiens is recorded. Every person is born with an individual program and three manipulation modes; this can be defined as "software," based on which he lives, and on the basis of which all his psychophysiology functions.

Since all research related to the Catalog of human population was and is being carried out within a strictly scientific framework, the following is the scientific definition: "The Catalog of human population is a description of a human as a type by subtype structures. Subtype structure (synonyms: "psyche", "soul") is a combination of individual archetypes, recorded at the genetic level (principle). Expressions and interaction of subtype structures in manipulation modes and phenological algorithms are described with adjustments for gender, age and cultural differences. Information is recorded on six factors." This definition was formulated and introduced by Andrey Davydov—the author of the discovery and decryption of the Catalog of human population.

3. Homo sapiens is a biological type divided into 293 subtypes.

The basis for cataloging of the "human" biological type was the discovery of existence of subtypes within this type. This discovery was made by the researcher-sinologist Andrey Davydov. It turned out that there are 293 subtypes of Homo sapiens. Each of them, using the language of science, is endemic. That is, representatives of one subtype cardinally differ from representatives of any other subtype due to particularities of arrangement and work of psychophysiology, qualities and characteristics, life algorithms, functional range, and abilities.

4. How does a representative of one human subtype of Homo sapiens differ from a representative of another subtype?

It has long been noted that even though people are physiologically similar in principle (for example, they have two arms, two legs, two lungs, one heart, and do not have scales, a tail, horns, hooves, wings, feathers, etc.), they differ from each other in character, qualities of personality, life algorithms, values, preferences, and abilities. And, sometimes they differ cardinally On the other hand, there are people, who are similar to one another. This question remained a mystery to researchers for a long time, but with the discovery of the Catalog of human population it was resolved. It turned out that the reason is that humanity as a biological type is divided into subtypes.

It is exactly the same as it is arranged in the world of animals, birds, fish, plants, etc. Among birds exist hummingbirds, and eagles, and sparrows, and ostriches; among fish there is a shark, and a carp, and a guppy or a dwarf pygmy goby; among snakes there are anacondas, and vipers, and grass snakes; among dogs there are huge Great Danes, and miniature Italian Greyhounds. And, as it is known, anacondas do not live like vipers, sharks like carps, and Great Danes like Italian Greyhounds—they all lead different lifestyles, have different qualities, functionalities, and abilities. As it turned out, it is the same within the biological type Homo sapiens.

5. How does one individual differ from another, as representatives of the same subtype of Homo sapiens?

In principle, they do not differ in anything. Externally, representatives of the same human subtype, unlike animals of the same subtype, might differ, including by the color of their skin, for example. However, they have the same qualities of personality, lifestyle, abilities, and functionalities. Despite that externally representatives of one subtype of biological type "human" usually do not look similar, their internal physiological processes are analogous. For example, if we consider the possibility of normal existence in different temperature regimes, then that what is natural and desirable for a representative of one human subtype might be completely unacceptable to a representative of another, etc.

This occurs because all physiological processes are determined by the structure of psyche, and it is identical for all representatives of one human subtype. Representatives of the same subtype of Homo sapiens are born with the same subtype program, and therefore, in terms of psychical structure they are identical. The structure of psyche (subtype program) is a natural imprint, a matrix, and it does not change from individual to individual within a subtype.

Social environment, upbringing, cultural traditions, and education introduce some adjustments, but they are minor since they do not change the essential—subtype structure ("program") of a person. Real differences between people are defined specifically by the natural subtype program, nothing else.

The study of Shan Hai Jing revealed that every person, belonging to some subtype, has stable characteristic properties of this subtype; and, regardless of race, nationality, place of birth and residence, parental guidance, and so on, as these are only minor correctors, which do not change a subtype program. Though, the same pattern is observed with animals. Living in different areas (as some animal subspecies, as well as human subspecies can be found almost all over the globe), the representatives of the same subtype may have different adaptive properties, but these properties do not in any way alter the subtype program: a horse remains a horse, a bear remains a bear, a bull does not turn into a ram, and a snake does not become a crocodile. Only here it will be a pony, somewhere else a percheron, and elsewhere—an Arabian horse. Regardless of the territory where an animal lives, it retains stable properties of its subtype. We see a similar situation with humans: the representatives of the same human subtype might have different skin color, be of different nationalities, but each retains those personal qualities, life algorithms, preferences, talents, functioning that are inherent in his subtype.

Cultural factors, national traditions, even parental upbringing (which, by the way, plays a big role for representatives of some subtypes) are only additions, layers, and do not alter the subtype program of a human. Since, in the case of biological species Homo sapiens, children are not direct continuation of their parents, as it is the case with animals. More often than not, children and parents are members of different subtypes.

6. Why and in which cases children are not antenna-like continuations of their biological parents?

As it turned out with the discovery of the Catalog of human population—since humanity as a biological type is divided into 293 subtypes, having a purely external similarity ("exterior") a child does not inherit natural psychophysiological characteristics of his biological parents, except for when he is a representative of the same subtype as one of his parents (a mother or a father).

In the case of representatives of the biological type "human," children are not antenna-like continuations of their biological parents, as it is the case in the world of animals and plants. In the world of Homo sapiens in most cases parents raise a representative or representatives who are not the same as their own subtype. This is the root cause of the well-known "problem of parents and children." This is why children, even though they resemble their parents externally, in most cases do not get all characteristics and qualities of their characters, do not copy their way of life exactly as it happens in the animal world. And, sometimes they cardinally differ from their parents by nature.

As for similarity of characters, habits, attitudes, etc. observed in parents and children—this has nothing to do with their nature, and is only related to artificial "software." We have fully researched this issue and it is described using popular language in the book titled Ahnenerbe—Your Killer Is Under Your Skin by A. Davydov and O. Skorbatyuk (also available in Part 3 of this book).

7. *Homo sapiens* is a bio-robot.

Using scientific terminology, Homo sapiens is a bio-form that has a program on the basis of which it functions in space and time, just like all other bio-forms on planet Earth. In other words, a human is the same bio-robot as all other natural objects.

A human, first of all, is a natural object, an element of the unified natural system. Any animal or plant lives and functions within strict programs. And, our planet itself and other elements of the Solar system are not able to move in space arbitrarily, deviate from their orbits; meaning that they are objects, which are programmed from the beginning.

A human is subject to the same natural laws. Subtype program of Homo sapiens gets activated at the moment of birth of an individual. And, he begins to live strictly according to this program, even if he knows nothing about it. It is the same as it is with, for example, animals and plants, or planets of the Solar system: Earth does not "visit" the orbit of Mars, a fish is not able to arbitrarily begin to live and function like a horse, and an oak cannot stop being an oak and begin to exist like a palm tree.

8. *Homo sapiens* is born with built-in "software": individual (subtype) program and three manipulation modes.

In essence, the concept of human "software" (or, using scientific terms—"subtype structure" or "individual archetypal pattern"), "psyche," and "soul" are synonymous. The role of human "software" is huge. It is the basis of work of all human psychophysiology.

Human "software" is the natural subtype program of an individual and three manipulation modes as correctors to this program: suppression mode, balance mode and stimulation mode. A program and three manipulation modes are "soldered together," as elements of a unified system called "human psyche." Every human subtype has its own, unique natural program with three manipulation modes. More information about programs and manipulation modes of Homo sapiens will be provided below.

Human "software," using the computer terms, gets "installed" by nature at the time of birth. If we draw an analogy with other technics, an individual program and three manipulation modes of a person are, relatively speaking, "factory settings," meaning that an individual is created by nature specifically like that.

9. Natural and artificial "software" of *Homo sapiens*.

A human and a computer have a similarity: both do not work without software. A computer without "software" is a useless pile of metal; a human without "software" is a body, life in which is supported by automatic physiological processes, but he will never function like a human. Today almost everyone is familiar with computer software, but not many are familiar with human "software." Even though, as it turned out, human "software" is the "soul," which people were looking for so hard for centuries, but could not find.

Human "software" can be natural, as well as artificially created by people themselves.

Nature gives "software" to every person from birth as a base, without which any bio-robot, including a human, cannot live. Without even coming close to that natural "software" is provided by nature to every person from birth, civilization came up with a lot of modifications of artificial "software." People had to live somehow since by nature it is arranged so that a person cannot live without a program at all, and the Catalog human population, where every person could find out his natural program was lost.

However, the trouble is that artificial "software" (meaning, "software" invented by people) differs from natural in the same way as plastic apples differ from natural apples. That is not surprising because even at the current level of technological development of this civilization, a human is not able to create anything that would be equal to natural; quality of that what he creates is always worse. Let's go back to "plastic apples": such a "diet" quickly leads to death of a human. In this civilization, in the best case, people live for several decades, instead of centuries, as they could live according to studies done by physiologists.

In essence, life based on artificial "software" that replaces the natural program of an individual, turns him into a living corpse while he is still alive. Life on artificial "software" leads to colossally rapid deterioration of the entire human psychophysiology, premature aging and early death. Only a few percent of the potential that is implanted in a person (and, which would allow him to heal and rejuvenate himself) gets realized and a person has nothing else left, but to die from diseases and old age.

And, during the time period between birth and death, for the most part, a person's life is difficult, full of problems. Is it not this process and result that are described in mythologies of almost all nations of the world: a shift from the Golden Age, in which all people lived for many years, happily and without problems to the Iron Age, tainted and cruel, when "men never rest from labour and sorrow by day, and from perishing by night"[1]?

Artificial "software," like hydrochloric acid, corrodes a person from the inside. As it is known, concentrated hydrochloric acid turns contents of a stomach into a bloody mess. A chemical burn of this kind does not always end instantaneously, sometimes doctors save a person by removing the insides, but a person lives the rest of his life severely disabled and dies before his time. And, at any stage a person is in hellish pain because of this. Is this not the same process that we can observe around us: life in misery, and then death, in 100% out of 100 cases?

No person in his lifetime is able to fall outside the scope of his natural program without damage to himself. And, everything that Homo sapiens try to make out of themselves by creating artificial programs, as replacements of their natural programs, in terms of nature are mutations. In nature all mutants automatically "go under the knife." Automatically—means that if functioning of an individual falls outside the scope of his natural program, then nature automatically regards this as a threat to existence of the whole natural system, and the program of self-destruction automatically turns on in that individual.

Probably, this is why lives of Homo sapiens in this civilization are so short. After all, according to physiologists—by nature a human body is designed for a healthy, normal and youthful life of a few hundred years. And, this is confirmed by the ancient sources; for example, in descriptions of lives of

biblical characters, which most people are familiar with. One of them—
Methuselah—lived 969 years according to some sources. Or is the Bible
wrong?

Artificial "software" is the root of absolutely any problem of an individual,
as well as society as a whole. "Software" created by a human for himself and
for other people can be compared to the most dangerous computer virus,
which breaks the entire system; to a virus, which there is not a single
chance to get rid of, except for doing "a factory reset," cleaning "the disk"
called "the soul" of everything extraneous, everything that is not related to
the natural "software." And, today this is possible since the Catalog of
human population, which is the collection of descriptions of human
programs, was found and returned to civilization.

Artificial schemes that people come up with as programs for life are unable
to completely turn off their natural "software." Simultaneous work of both
natural and artificial "software," first of all, makes the life of an individual
very uncomfortable, as these two "programs" come into a conflict, which
does not end until death. Secondly, this is very similar to trying to sit on two
chairs at once. And, the result is the same. Trying to resolve this conflict,
but not knowing his natural program, at some point an individual
completely switches over to artificial "software." The trouble is that when he
"succeeds"—he dies right away; a person is alive only while his natural
program works. Therefore, natural "software" of people, which is described
in the Catalog of human population, always corresponds to real people.
And, this is easily observable.

1 Hesiod [VII-VII century BC]. Works and Days. Retrieved March 14, 2015
from http://www.sacred-texts.com/cla/hesiod/works.htm.

10. Why know the natural individual (subtype) program of a human?

Characteristics of species and subspecies of animals and plants, which are
different by nature, make it possible to classify and describe them in
encyclopedias. This, in turn, allows a person to obtain information about a
certain natural object or phenomenon from encyclopedias, reference books
and other catalogs. For example, from catalogs of animals—it is possible to
learn the natural qualities of each of them, how they look, how they live,
what they eat, how they reproduce, etc.

Prior to creation of such catalogs, a human had to learn this "on his own
skin." Encyclopedias (catalogs), which describe the world of nature, relieved

people from having to learn on their own that some animals can damage or even kill, that plants can be very poisonous, and that water in nature is not only a brook or a calmly flowing river, but also vertiginous currents, swamps that suck in deep, huge ocean waves, floods, etc.

Without an encyclopedia, from which it is possible to easily find out about any person, the same thing happens to those, who without having knowledge about the true nature of their fellow biological species try to come into contact with them. People's lives are full of troubles, dangers and damages because they do not know qualities and functionalities of people with whom they communicate.

After all, as it turned out, human natural programs are a mix of properties of real objects of nature: animals, plants, mountains, valleys, rivers, lakes, swamps, streams, rocks, minerals, soils, metals, and much more. And, among them there are not only peaceful rabbits or sparrows, but also tigers, wild boars, venomous snakes or insects; not only quiet rivers and lakes, but also rapidly flowing streams; not only carps, but piranhas and sharks; not only buttercups and daisies, but plants, like, for example, manchineel or Cerberus. And, for example, without knowledge of natural properties of manchineel, if a person hides under its branches from the rain—drops with mixed-in poisonous milky sap will fall from the tree onto that person, and he will become covered with blisters from head to toe.

Therefore, without the Catalog of human population every person has a lot of problems throughout life. These problems never end because he is always among people. And, people in this civilization do everything to hide their true qualities of personality, their natural functionalities behind numerous cover ups and masks. Under the guise of a white lamb or a beautiful flower can hide anyone and anything. As a result, figuratively speaking, a person without knowledge of individual (subtype) programs of other people, first steps on the tail of a poisonous snake and it bites him, then gets sucked into a swamp, then a rock hits him on the head, then he gets ripped by poisonous thorns, then he finds himself in a tornado zone or even paws of a tiger.

For a long time Homo sapiens remained one of the few biological objects, which was not arranged systematically by subtype structures in an encyclopedia. Of course, some encyclopedias about a human existed, for example, anatomical atlases. However, one could not get information about what this or that person is like, let alone how to come into contact, interact with him. But now the biological type "human" is classified due to that researcher-sinologist A. Davydov discovered detailed descriptions of two hundred and ninety three human subtypes in the ancient monument titled Shan Hai Jing, which is why this book was named the Catalog of human population.

The Catalog of human population is an encyclopedia of Homo sapiens, from which it is possible to obtain detailed descriptions of people. From this directory one can easily find out the natural individual (subtype) program of any of over 7 billion people living on planet Earth.

Consideration of each person as a representative of one of the subtypes allows to find out any information about him/her using minimal form data, only by the date of his/her birth. This is very convenient.

The Catalog of human population allows to obtain any information about a person on all six factors: what this person is like in the intellectual sphere, how he/she thinks, at what rate and in which algorithms, what his/her interests are, etc.; what, when, where and how he/she eats; what are his/her physical parameters, abilities, etc.; what emotional manifestations are normal for him/her, how powerful they are, how and in which situations he/she expresses emotions, etc.; what are his/her sexual preferences, sexual potential, how it gets expressed, in what forms, with which partners, under what conditions and algorithms, etc.; in what geographical area, type of housing, interior, conditions he/she prefers to live; what his/her natural talents are, how they can be realized (including professional activity, although not necessarily); how he/she communicates with others, on what bases, what he/she seeks, by which methods, and what other people should be fearful of with him/her; and so on.

To know the natural individual (subtype) program of a person means to know all his/her hidden "motivational springs," personality traits, life algorithms, functions, abilities, habits, and predilections; including everything that an individual usually carefully hides from others. This knowledge fully reveals the true nature of a person (which is usually hidden behind numerous masks), giving a complete picture of who he or she is— real, "without embellishments."

In order to make contact with another person and turn it in the needed direction, it is necessary to understand exactly who your opponent is: how he/she will act, what and how he/she will say, what he/she will seek, and so on. To know all this, it is no longer necessary to meet up with this person, to observe him, to try to learn something about him from someone, to provoke some actions, to study his reactions, and so on. There is no longer a need to be in any situation with a person in order to know exactly what to expect from him (what actions, what reactions, what decisions) and what to be cautious of with him. It is enough to simply read the description of a person in the Catalog of human population.

It is possible to read any type of information about any person in Catalog of human population. It is just as easy as learning, for example, about dogs from a reference book about dogs. And, this is at a minimum because the Catalog of human population also contains information about how to make a person absolutely controllable from the outside, about how he should "grow," meaning—gradually develop, self-perfect, etc.

11 What is the natural individual (subtype) program of *Homo sapiens*?'

Individual (subtype) program of Homo sapiens is a program, based on which a person lives. He is unable to go beyond it. A program "starts up" and begins to work at the time of birth; to be more precise, at the time of cutting of the umbilical cord.

Individual program of a person is a program of one of 293 human subtypes. Therefore, we use the term "individual (subtype) program." The program of each subtype differs from programs of all other subtypes.

An individual (subtype) program is recorded in human unconscious by the language of natural images (archetypes). Archetypes are a protolanguage. Unconscious of Homo sapiens "speaks" this language and human psychophysiology "understands" only this language. One human program can contain about 20 or over 100 natural images. Individual programs of human subtypes are recorded by different quantities of images, but no subtype has any advantages over other subtypes—all have equal potential and survival rate.

Each individual (subtype) program consists of two parts "active" and "passive."

Each individual (subtype) program is described in the Catalog of human population on six factors: intellectual, physical, nutritional, emotional, sexual, and environmental.

Appearance of people with various subtype programs is connected with natural phenological cycles. Therefore, it is necessary to know the day, month, and year of birth of a person in order to find his description in Shan Hai Jing.

12. How an individual (subtype) program of a person is connected with his/her date of birth?

It is necessary to know the day, month and year of birth of a person in order to find his/her description in the Catalog of human population. However, we have to disappoint astrology and numerology fans, as this is not related to influence of planets and stars, or "magic of numbers." This is related to natural phenological cycles.

For those who are not familiar with the science called "phenology"—in a nutshell, it is a system of knowledge and sets of information about seasonal phenomena of nature, time periods of their occurrences and reasons that define these periods, as well as the science of space-time laws of cyclical changes of natural objects and their complexes, associated with annual movement of the Earth around the Sun.

In nature, absolutely all bio-forms (plants, animals, birds, fish, insects, reptiles, etc.) appear during their time periods. Scientists have recorded this fact a long time ago. At the beginning of the last century, a German zoologist Alfred Brehm has demonstrated that each type of living organism appears on earth during a specific time period.

For example, rabbits are born in late April-early May, deer—in May-June, seals—in March, and so on. "...And the stork in the heaven knoweth the appointed times, and the turtle, and the swallow and the crane observe the time of their coming..." (Jeremiah 8:7) A human, as part of the earth's ecosystem, as part of nature is subject to the same laws as all other natural objects; therefore, if at certain specific time periods creatures, which we call "a cow", "an eagle" or "a hippopotamus" are born, then exactly the same rule applies to a human.

Using scientific terminology, Homo sapiens is programmed bio-form, anthropo-zoomorphic being, individual (subtype) archetypal pattern of which depends on phenological cycling of a geographical area. Appearance of subtypes of the biological type Homo sapiens is connected with natural phenological cycles, and specifically for this reason, classification of subtypes in the Catalog of human population is recorded according to the date of birth.

Andrey Davydov—the author of the discovery of the Catalog of human population in the ancient Chinese monument Shan Hai Jing, and the author of creation of the technology of decryption of this ancient monument—put together a schedule of appearance of subtype structures of type human, and this schedule is copyrighted.

13. How 293 individual subtype programs are distributed if there are 365 or 366 (leap years) days in a year?

Despite the fact that birth of a particular subtype structure is firmly connected to the date of birth, in the case of research of the ancient monument Shan Hai Jing (which turned out to be the Catalog of human population) things are not as simple as they are in astrology. At least because there are 365 days in a year (or 366 in leap year), while there are 293 subtype structures of Homo sapiens described in the Book of

Mountains and Seas. However, this problem has long been solved by Andrey Davydov—the author of the scientific discovery of the Catalog.

However, many of those who learn about the Catalog are concerned about the question of how 293 individual subtype programs are distributed if there are 365 or 366 (leap years) days in a year. We uncovered that some subtype programs are reproduced a few days in a row. However, this does not mean that people born in this period are absolutely the same because manipulation modes of these individual programs are often completely different. Therefore, to put it in simple terms, these people are not like each other one hundred percent, but they do share the same subtype program— meaning, individual qualities and algorithms.

14. When does a human subtype program turn on?

"Hour X," as time of birth of a human, starts up his subtype program. The "soul" begins to work, and a human—to live. And, he will live while his soul, in other words—his subtype program as a mechanism works in his body, and works on all six factors: intellect, physiology, nutrition, emotions, sexual factor and environmental factor. If the work of one of these factors stops, then breakage of other factors will follow: fast, as in the case of, for example, physical and nutritional factors (starvation, disease), or slow, as, for example, in the case of sexual, emotional or intellectual factors.

It does not matter how a person was born, whether in a natural way or, for example, with the use of cesarean section. Individual subtype program starts working at the moment of cutting of the umbilical cord. It does not matter when a person was conceived, how long the pregnancy lasted, and so on. The only important moment is the time of detachment of his body from the body of his mother in the form of cutting of the umbilical cord because that is the moment when the individual (subtype) program begins to work.

There is a supposition (although we have not studied this issue within interdisciplinary research) that subtype programs of Homo sapiens is the record that human DNA contains. It is very likely that every human embryo initially contains a record of all 293 subtype structures, along with manipulation modes for each one of them and a record of passage through these stages of personal (subtype) evolution of an individual, which are also programmed and are described in Shan Hai Jing. This is a huge array of information. However, at the moment of birth only one of the subtype structures is activated, and all other records remain inactivated. Once again, unlike everything else presented here, this is only a hypothesis.

15. Is it necessary to know the time of birth besides the day, month and year of birth of a person in order to find his/her description in the Catalog of human population?

This information is required only when there is data that a person was born close to midnight—half an hour before midnight, or within a half hour after midnight. In this case, special technology is used to determine where the description of this person is located in the Catalog of Mountains and Seas. As for the time of birth within one 24 hour period—this factor does not matter for finding a description of a person in the Catalog of human population.

16. Why is it necessary to have accurate information about the year of birth of a person?

It is very important to know the year of birth of a person in order to get information about him/her from the Catalog of human population. It is important to know the year for one reason only: to understand whether it is a leap year or a common year. Since in most cases if two people were born on the same day, but one of them was born in a common year and the other was born in a leap years, then they are representatives of different human subtypes. Therefore, they have different individual (subtype) programs and manipulations modes. In this case, they have completely different qualities, characteristics and functions, they lead different lifestyles.

Of course, coincidences do happen because the ancient monument Shan Hai Jing contains 293 descriptions of human programs and, as it is known, there are 365 days in a year. However, in order to use this information, it is necessary to know exactly which programs are reproduced multiples times.

Therefore, without having knowledge of the exact year of birth of the person of interest—accurate information from the Catalog of human population about this person cannot be obtained. However, this is not a problem because in the modern world it is very easy to get information about when a person was born. Usually, it does not even cross a person's mind to hide this kind of information about himself. Also, it is easy to find it in public records, profiles in social networks, documents, forms, and so on.

17. What are "Active" and "Passive" of an individual (subtype) program of a person?

As it turned out, any natural program of Homo sapiens, regardless of subtype, consists of two parts. The author of this scientific discovery, researcher-sinologist Andrey Davydov named these parts "Active" and "Passive."

The "Active" part of a human program is responsible for the period of a person's activity. It is a period of real actions, but also a period of active energy and strength expenditure. Therefore, every person requires rest from time to time, and not only in the form of sleep, but also in the form of some type of activity. Not for nothing there exists a saying: "The best rest is change of activity." Human activities from the "Passive" part of his individual program do not take away strength, but rather help a person accumulate it, turn on regeneration processes in him.

Not knowing about the existence of this natural mechanism, which is built into every human, people are often frightened of that two different personalities are always present in others or in themselves all the time. The diagnosis known as "dissociative identity disorder" does not require any treatment, if we do not consider clinical cases in the field of psychiatry when, using the language of Non-traditional Psychoanalysis, a serious malfunction of the individual (subtype) program occurs.

"Active" and "Passive," to put it very raspingly and primitively—are like two different human characters because each part of the human program is recorded by different images, which give a different character, style of actions of a person, and algorithms of his life. In practice, this manifests in the so-called duality of any person. For example: Mr. N is quiet and harmless at work, but at home he is active, loud, and despotic; a different Mr. N uses his intellect at work as an analyst, and during the time of rest chooses physical exercise and, as they say, "does not use his head at all;" some other Mr. N behaves as a leader in communication with several people, but when he is with only one other person—he completely subjects to another's will; and so on and so forth. There are many examples, but the main thing here is that every person (a man or a woman) is "dual" by nature, double-natured. This "duality" is necessary because one cannot be passively recovering while simultaneously actively spending himself.

Existence of separation of individual (subtype) programs into "Active" and "Passive," in our view, can be explained by the fact that sometimes twins have different characters, habits, functionality, qualities of personality. Without getting into details, we will just say that according to our observations, in some cases twins can share a single subtype program; meaning that one lives according to the "Active" part of the program, and the other on the basis of the "Passive." We do not know yet why this happens, more research needs to be done on this, but this fact is the reason twins differ in their personal qualities, characters, algorithms and so on, even though both twins belong to the same subtype.

18. What are "six factors of a human?"

In the Catalog of human population, which is compiled on the basis of decryption of the ancient monument Shan Hai Jing, all information about a person consists of a general description of an individual and a description of his qualities and functioning on six factors.

Classification by six factors, which are fundamentally different from each other, is a system created by researcher-sinologist Andrey Davydov to describe functioning of human subtypes during compilation of the Catalog of human population. Since at a certain point he was faced with a problem: how to structure information obtained from the ancient source about a particular subtype in descriptions of psychophysiological diapason of a subtype? Data obtained from the ancient text contained very diverse information about a human: how representatives of a particular human subtype think, data about their nutritional or environmental diapason, sexual peculiarities, and so on.

In fields that are traditionally related to a human (for example, in medicine) no systems were found, according to which to would be possible to distribute information obtained from Shan Hai Jing. It was necessary to create a classification, which would encompass human life activity in general. To solve this problem, Andrey Davydov identified six factors: intellectual, physical, nutritional, emotional, sexual, and environmental.

And, as it is easy to notice, intellectual factor is only a part of human psyche, and not the most important one. Not to appear unfounded, we will provide an example. If there is certain influence on the physical factor of a human (for example, induction of a painful shock), or influence on the nutritional factor (for example, leaving a person without food or drink for a long time), or influence in a way that a person begins to experience a strong sexual arousal or a strong emotional stress—then, his intellectual factor will turn off, and he will function on the basis of instincts, reflexes, automated processes in his organism. Even a severe headache, as one of the states of the human physical factor, can partially disable the intellect, meaning that a person's thought process will be quite unproductive. Therefore, it was concluded that the intellectual factor is only one of six factors of human psychophysiology.

19. Why six factors, and not more?

Number of factors to describe primary programs could not be expanded, supplemented by some other factor. Despite a common misconception that at the first level of development Homo sapiens has so-called "spirituality"— information from the ancient text did not confirm this. The appearance of the factor of "spirituality" in humans is a separate topic.

20. What is the difference between a woman's and a man's natural program within one subtype?

Men and women within one human subtype differ from each other in the same way as females and males within one subspecies of, for example, animals. They have identical personal characteristics, psychophysiological algorithms, lifestyle, and functionality. Some differences might be present in the sexual factor; for example, in attitudes towards offspring. In nature, females of some species of animals care for their offspring without participation of males; females make males leave their offspring; not only males, but also females of some species do not engage in caring for their offspring at all; or, for example, a male and a female of some types of birds engage in upbringing of their nestlings together and distribute parenting duties equally. However, as mentioned above, these differences are not fundamental.

APPENDIX A

INFORMATION FROM THE CATALOG OF HUMAN POPULATION (CATALOG OF HUMAN SOULS)

What Are *Human Programs* And *Manipulation Modes*?

Each person (*Homo sapiens*) is a bio-robot with an individual program (or software). Without an operating system (software) a computer cannot function; without a program, a person too does not function. The human program is a set of main functions that allows management of all psycho-physiology of a person. The program distinguishes one *Homo sapiens* from another.

Manipulation modes are modes of regulation of an individual program (operating software) of a person. Each and every single individual human program is a system, which can be managed from the outside or can be managed by oneself. Three manipulation modes are correction modes of an individual program. If you know these correction modes of a person and transmit them, use them on the outside then the person is controlled by you. By knowing each other's subconscious motivations this tool can be used consciously. Since all models of psyche are described in the *Catalog of Human Population (Catalog Of Human Souls)*, then it is understood that humans are programmed beings and are bio-robots (bio-robots because the form is alive, but programmed by Nature).

Since it is now understood that every person is a bio-robot with a program and manipulation modes - it is possible to assume that only one thing is ethical: NOT TO BREAK the PROGRAM, but to correctly treat, interact with a person – that is ethics. Often one does not even know what one is capable of, what one was born for, what qualities one possesses since birth.

Often, not realizing what these qualities are and not understanding how one could apply them, the person's potential is not used throughout their life.

If someone has no specific knowledge about personal qualities and abilities, it is possible that that person will spend their whole life trying "to find him/herself" "to find a place in life". However, in the end, a person does not find and does not realize them because: (1) it is an unrealistic task to try yourself in all spheres of life, and (2) one is strongly influenced by external conditions.

However, from the Laboratory's point of view–the program of any person is primary (an individual program of a person is their own operating software). People got used to adapting to external conditions, but their subtype programs demand their own. The result is that everywhere we run into absolutely unimaginable situations, which occur because of collisions of the above-stated: demands of the environment and requirements of the program of a person.

The goal of those studying the *Catalog of Human Population / Catalog of Human Souls* (the laws of Nature, described in this ancient source, *Shan Hai Jing*, which was left to us by our Creators) is to comprehend the laws of Nature as much as possible, to live by them and not to break them. Only this ensures survival of any subtype structure, because Nature does not care if you are concerned about it or your program, whether you understand it or not; Nature does not lose anything when people (bio-robots) die. Nature is wise - it simply replaces one body that has a certain subtype program with another.

If a person does not strive for survival they perish. That is natural selection. Those who study the *Catalog of Human Population (Catalog of Human Souls)*, try to understand Nature because they want to increase their survival and success rates. What you choose is only up to you.

What Is A Decryption Of A Human Program?

All human programs are recorded in an ancient language in the manuscript called *The Collection of Mountains and Seas*. There are about 300 individual human subtype structures, and their decryption is the main intellectual product of the Laboratory. The decryption of a program is a description of properties, qualities and peculiarities of a person (a complete psychological portrait of a person) and their functions according to *six factors*:

* the **intellectual factor**, which accumulates information that characterizes the power of intelligence, ability to generate information, process and generate ideas, perform analytic work, etc.
* the **physical factor**, which includes information related to the perception of physical attributes, hygiene, field of application, as well as textures, color characteristics, clothing, etc.
* the **dietological (or nutritional) factor**, which summarizes information regarding preferences for particular foods, frequency and form of consumption and so on.
* the **emotional factor**, which incorporates information on emotional algorithms (Note: emotions are a source of energy and are required for normal function of psycho-physiology).
* the **sexual factor**, which includes data on the power of potency, frequency, types of sexual relations, the choice for monogamy and/or polygamy, sexual orientation, views on having children, etc.
* the **environmental factor**, which includes facts regarding education, profession, career choice, as well as migration and other processes.

What Are The Three Manipulation/Regulation Modes Of A Person?

Any person has a program and three manipulation modes. Manipulation modes are correction modes of the psyche and physiology of an individual. Inside of a system (a human), they act as modes of self-control which work on "automatic." Being translated from the outside, they turn into a control tool, one that allows anyone to get complete power over a person without dependence from his will as the translation of manipulation modes does not get registered by the intellect and consciousness of the receiver.

Three manipulation modes of any person are:

Suppression Mode: or the pleasure mode, which turns off the will of a person and is capable of stopping any of his activities, forcing the individual to submit to the manipulator, to love him, worship him, etc. Translation of the suppression mode of an individual by a manipulator means love, pleasure, realization of a dream, or happiness for that individual.

Balance Mode: comfort mode and balance mode of the psycho-physiology of an individual; carriers of this mode are perceived as friends. Translations of the balance mode of an individual by a manipulator means friendship, mutual understanding, or identical opinions.

Stimulation Mode: a mode that causes irritation, hatred and aversion; serves as the "act now" button for the program. Translations of the stimulation mode of an individual by a manipulator means irritation as the stimulus for action, hostility and more.

What Is A Decryption Of A Manipulation Mode Of A Human?

Manipulation modes are recorded in an ancient language in the manuscript called *The Collection of Mountains and Seas*. Decryptions of three manipulation modes of a human are provided in the form of three descriptions, based on the six factors (intellectual, physical, dietological (nutritional), emotional, sexual and environmental), and describe a system of self-regulation (control) of an individual.

What Are Images Of A Program And Manipulation Modes Of A Person?

All human programs and manipulation modes were recorded in the *Collection of Mountains and Seas* using images. These images are an ancient language that scientists have decoded. The images give a human those precise properties, qualities and functions that are presented in the decryptions. A human program is a set of basic functions that allow the management of all psycho-physiology of a person, while every image of a program is one of these functions.

Using computer language, an image is a part of an operational system of a human, responsible for its functionality. Images, like an interface, provide an interaction between the physiology and psyche of a person. The description of any person surpasses volumes of the well-known *Encyclopædia Britannica*, which comprises a total of 32 volumes in its 15th edition. Due to the large quantity (nearly 300) of human subtypes that exist in Nature and are described in the *Collection of Mountains and Seas*, researchers provide just the most basic information in their decryptions.

However, if a person knows the images by which this or that program (or mode) is recorded, then the information can be expanded further, independently. You can expand a decryption using encyclopedias on Nature, mythological directories, etc. If you know your images, you can do this by yourself, or you can receive professional help on how to study your images via individual consultations.

What Are Birth Dates Of Manipulation Modes Carriers?

Every person is a carrier of a certain program. They self-regulate (or are regulated by someone) using the three manipulation modes. (Every subtype structure has its own 3 manipulation modes.) Any manipulation mode is someone's individual program.

APPENDIX B

BENEFITS OF INFORMATION FROM THE CATALOG OF HUMAN POPULATION (CATALOG OF HUMAN SOULS)

Benefits Of Information About Your Subtype Program

❖ Reception of answers to questions such as "Who am I? What am I? What is my purpose? How should I live? Why do I live like this, and not that?" People no longer need to direct these questions towards society, only to receive confusing answers that have nothing to do with reality. With their new-found time and energy, the person can now spend them on anything, including self-realization.

❖ The opportunity to be a genius, an outstanding person not only in your dreams.

❖ A precise understanding of what is yours, and what is not. An opportunity to cut-off those recommendations and influences from the external world, that destroy you physically and mentally.

❖ An improved quality of life, which begins to bring pleasure and joy, becomes interesting, full, bright, and finally makes sense.

❖ The person becomes stronger, healthier, wiser, more vigorous, more powerful, more competitive, more sexual, etc. He starts to significantly surpass himself as well as his associates as he compares himself to the way he was before his became familiar with his program.

❖ The person begins to understand the reasons behind his actions and gets a chance to live not "automatically," but consciously.

❖ The increase of your cultural level, and an increase of your survival rate in your environment. Culture is the basis for the survival rate of an individual in both social and natural environments.

❖ The *Catalog of Human Population (Catalog Of Human Souls)* is the only existing source in the civilization of individual ways of development capable of making a bio-robot become a Human.

Benefits of Information About Someone Else's Program

❖ Learn what the other person really is, learn to be able to see "inside," beyond the "façade," to understand who you are truly dealing with.
❖ Learn to precisely understand the motivational mechanisms of another person that force them to act.
❖ Learn to predict someone else's behavior.
❖ Learn to understand what to expect or demand from another, and what not to, because nobody is capable of going beyond their own program.
❖ Learn to precisely calculate how, in what areas and by what means to most effectively use any given human resource.
❖ Learn to establish ideal communication.

Benefits Of Information About Your Manipulation/Regulation Modes

❖ It allows complete self-control.
❖ It provides a clear understanding of what exactly makes you submit, and allows you to stop being manipulated by others.

Benefits Of Information About Someone Else's Manipulation Modes

❖ The ability to have full control over that person.
❖ An ideal tool in the process of communication, since there is an opportunity to speak someone else's language, to be heard and understood.
❖ The ability to form any attitude towards you (respect, love, hatred, friendly feelings, feelings of a worship, etc.).

❖ It allows you to build any type of relationship with another person.

Benefits Of Knowing Your Or Someone Else's Images

❖ Receive visual information (in the form of images, or pictures) about yourself or someone else.
❖ Know who you really are.
❖ The given information is easily perceived and acquired by the subconscious.
❖ Understand where qualities and someone else's life algorithms provided in a description are taken from.
❖ Gain access to an enormous volume of information about a person: by studying an image(s), it is possible to independently add data to the decoding of a program or a manipulation mode.

Benefits Of Having Birth Dates Of Your Manipulation Modes Carriers

❖ Find living carriers of your modes in your environment, look at them, compare them to the description, etc.
❖ Feel their influence on your psycho-physiology.
❖ Communicate to these people for any purposes (friendship, partnership, sex, management, business, creation of family, research interests, etc.).
❖ Communicate with people who really understand you and are truly close to you.

APPENDIX C

SOME OF THE CONSEQUENCES OF APPLICATION OF THE CATALOG OF HUMAN POPULATION (CATALOG OF HUMAN SOULS)

Technological Consequences

If, in the organic world to which animals and plants belong, it is possible to consider plants and animals as bio-forms with an operating system based on the classification they are in, then a person can also be considered part of this world programmed by Nature. It enables one to take a cybernetic approach to a person and use him/her as the base (instead of hi-tech material objects) in communication processes.

Social Consequences

If we recognize that the main resource of a civilization is an individual, his possibilities, and his characteristics, a more adequate use of this resource (human) can give a more purposeful vector of development for a civilization. Moreover, in the following model "Universe–Earth–Human"--a human, with the help of our technology, becomes the component that we know most about.

Economic Consequences

There is an opportunity to consider a person in manipulation modes, meaning naturally and artificially created scenarios. In them, a person can be put in subordinate or lead positions. Certain combinations will allow one to predict and create optimal, comfortable conditions for any person, which will be described in advance in a certain hierarchical scheme. When the given project is realized, it is possible to close "an empty spot" in modern science—cataloging (classification) of the human population. The given Catalog will contain information about the psycho-physiology of any person in manipulation modes. It answers modern research in the field of cybernetics, where a person is considered to be a cybernetic structure (a bio-robot). The given Catalog can also be considered as a Catalog of the software of every human subtype. This approach enables one to predict sales volume of the *Catalog of Human Population (Catalog Of Human Souls)* similar to the sales volume of software products by *Microsoft*.

OUR OTHER BOOKS RELATED TO OUR SCIENTIFIC RESEARCH

Monographic Series

Archetypal Pattern. Fundamentals of Non-Traditional Psychoanalysis.

Davydov, A., & Skorbatyuk, O. (2014). K. Bazilevsky (Ed.). Anonymous (Trans.). *Archetypal Pattern. Fundamentals of Non-Traditional Psychoanalysis: Vol. 1. From Carl Gustav Jung's Archetypes of the Collective Unconscious to Individual Archetypal Patterns.* (Composed 2005. Original work published 2013 in Russian, ISBN 9781301447688.). San Diego, CA: HPA Press. ISBN 9781311820082

Davydov, A., & Skorbatyuk, O. (2014). K. Bazilevsky (Trans.). *Archetypal Pattern. Fundamentals of Non-Traditional Psychoanalysis: Vol. 2. Can Archetypal Images Contain Chimeras?* (Composed 2005. Original work published 2013 in Russian, ISBN 978130184859.). San Diego, CA: HPA Press. ISBN 9781310658570

Davydov, A., & Skorbatyuk, O. (2014). Arkhetipicheskiy Pattern. Osnovy Netraditsionnogo Psikhoanaliza [Archetypal Pattern. Fundamentals of Non-Traditional Psychoanalysis]: *Vol. 3. Archetype Semantics: How This Corresponds to the Concept of an 'Image'. How Archetypal Are Images?* (Composed 2005.). Marina Del Rey, CA: Catalog Of Human Souls GP. ISBN 9781301337309

Davydov, A., & Skorbatyuk, O. (2014). K. Bazilevsky (Trans.). *Archetypal Pattern. Fundamentals of Non-Traditional Psychoanalysis: Vol. 4. Society As A Community Of Manipulators And Their Subjects.* (Composed 2005. Original work published 2013 in Russian, ISBN 9781301399901.). San Diego, CA: HPA Press. ISBN 9781311809353

Catalog of Human Population - Non-Fiction Series

Individual (Subtype) Human Programs

Davydov, A., & Skorbatyuk, O. (2013). *Katalog Chelovecheskikh Dush: Programmnoye Obespecheniye Dushi Muzhchin/Zhenshchin, Rodivshikhsya <Data>* [Catalog of Human Souls: Software of Soul of Men/Women Born On <Date>] (Vols. 1-218. In Russian. Composed 2005-

2013.). Marina Del Rey, CA: Catalog Of Human Souls GP. [Available at http://www.humanpopulationacademy.org/pricing/ in all languages].

Human Manipulation Modes

Davydov, A., & Skorbatyuk, O. (2013-2014). *Katalog Chelovecheskikh Dush: Kak Podchinit' Muzhchin/Zhenshchin, Rozhdonnykh <Data>. Zhenskiy/Muzhskoy Manipulyativnyy Ctsenariy.* [Catalog of Human Souls: How To Subdue Men/Women Born On <Date>. Female/Male Manipulation Scenario.] (Vols. 1-39. In Russian. Composed 2005-2013.). Marina Del Rey, CA: Catalog Of Human Souls GP. [Available at http://www.humanpopulationacademy.org/pricing/ in all languages].

Ideologies

Davydov, A. (2014). K. Bazilevsky (Trans.). *Terrorism: A Concept For The ATC (The Commonwealth Of Independent States Anti-Terrorism Center).* (Composed 2001. Original work published 2014 in Russian, ISBN 9781311277848.). San Diego, CA: HPA Press. ISBN 9781310032189

Davydov, A. (2014). K. Bazilevsky (Trans.). *Ideology Of Monarchy. For Office Of The Head Of The Russian Imperial House, Her Imperial Highness Grand Duchess Maria Vladimirovna.* (Composed 2003. Original work published 2014 in Russian, ISBN 9781310150340.). San Diego, CA: HPA Press. ISBN 9781311970152

Davydov, A., & Skorbatyuk, O. (2014). K. Bazilevsky (Trans.). *Ideology Of Religions. Scientific Proof Of Existence Of "God": The Catalog Of Human Population.* (Original work published 2014 in Russian, ISBN 9781311946690.). San Diego, CA: HPA Press. ISBN 9781311413932 ISBN 9780988648593

Political Science

Davydov, A. (2014). K. Bazilevsky (Trans.). *Essence Of Political Ideologies And Their Role In The Historical Process (Political History Of Russia).* (Composed 2003. Original work published 2014 in Russian, ISBN 9781310199929.). San Diego, CA: HPA Press. ISBN 9781310199929

Davydov, A. (2014). K. Bazilevsky (Trans.). *Influence Of Psychophysiological Specifics Of A Leader On The Style Of Political Decision-Making.* (Composed 2003. Original work published 2014 in Russian, ISBN 9781310037832). San Diego, CA: HPA Press. ISBN 9781310104558

Davydov, A. (2014). K. Bazilevsky (Trans.). *Elitist Political Concepts*. (Composed 2005. Original work published 2014 in Russian, ISBN 9781310223228). San Diego, CA: HPA Press. ISBN 9781310822858

General Non-Fiction

Bazilevsky, K. (2012). *Human Population Academy: Laws of Human Nature Based on Shan Hai Jing Research Discoveries by A. Davydov & O. Skorbatyuk*. San Diego, CA: HPA Press. ISBN 9781301986781 ISBN 9780988648500

Davydov, A. (2013). *Shan Khay Tszin: Mify Ili Struktura Psikhiki?* [Shan Hai Jing: Myths Or Structure Of Psyche?] (Composed 1999. Originally pub. 1999 in Russian in Moscow: *Power Of Spirit*, 32-35.). Marina Del Rey, CA: Catalog Of Human Souls GP. ISBN 9781301590391

Davydov, A. (2013). *"Shan Khay Tszin" i "I Tszin" – Karta Psikhofiziologicheskoy Struktury Cheloveka?* [Shan Hai Jing and I Ching – Map of Human Psychophysiological Structure?] (Composed 2002.). Marina Del Rey, CA: Catalog Of Human Souls GP. ISBN 9781301510009

Davydov, A., & Skorbatyuk, O. (2014). K. Bazilevsky (Trans.). *AHNENERBE: Your Killer Is Under Your Skin* (Original work published 2014 in Russian, ISBN 9781311356741.). San Diego, CA: HPA Press. ISBN 9781311266682

Catalog of Human Souls – Non-Fiction Series

Skorbatyuk, O., & Bazilevsky, K. (2015). *Catalog of Human Souls: Vol. 1. Homo Sapiens Are Bio-Robots. Human "Software."* (Original work published 2015 in Russian, ISBN 9781310973109.). San Diego, CA: HPA Press. ISBN 9781310865893 ISBN 9780996731201

Skorbatyuk, O., & Bazilevsky, K. (2015). *Catalog of Human Souls: Vol. 2. Hack anyone's soul. 100 Demos Of Human Programs From The Catalog Of Human Population.* (Original work published 2015 in Russian, ISBN 9781311815101.). San Diego, CA: HPA Press. ISBN 9781310984785 ISBN 9780996731218

Skorbatyuk, O., & Bazilevsky, K. (2015). *Catalog of Human Souls: Vol. 3. Human Manipulation Modes. Either You Are Manipulating*

Or You Are Being Manipulated. (Original work published 2015 in Russian, ISBN 9781310250521.). San Diego, CA: HPA Press. ISBN 9781311918598 ISBN 9780996731225

Davydov, A., & Skorbatyuk, O. (2015). K. Bazilevsky (Trans.). *Catalog of Human Souls: Vol. 4. Non-Traditional Psychoanalysis. Selected Scientific Articles And Presentations At Conferences.* (Original work published 2014 in Russian, ISBN 9781310498299.). San Diego, CA: HPA Press. ISBN 9781310750373 ISBN 9780996731232

Bazilevsky, K. (2015). *Catalog of Human Souls: Vol. 5. Shan Hai Jing—A Book Covered With Blood. The Story Of Developers Of The Catalog Of Human Population.* (Original work published 2014 in Russian, ISBN 9781310149979.). San Diego, CA: HPA Press. ISBN 9781310766732 ISBN 9780996731249

A Man And A Woman – Non-Fiction Series

A Log With Legs Spread Wide

Davydov, A., & Skorbatyuk, O. (2014). K. Bazilevsky (Trans.). *A Log With Legs Spread Wide: Vol. 1. How Men Turn Women Into Nothing.* (Original work published 2014 in Russian, ISBN 9781310388125.). San Diego, CA: HPA Press. ISBN 9781311155771

Davydov, A., & Skorbatyuk, O. (2014). K. Bazilevsky (Trans.). *A Log With Legs Spread Wide: Vol. 2. How Goddesses Are Turned Into Logs. World History Of Turning Women Into Mats.* (Original work published 2014 in Russian, ISBN 9781311238894.). San Diego, CA: HPA Press. ISBN 9781311915603

Davydov, A., & Skorbatyuk, O. (2013). *A Log With Legs Spread Wide: Vol. 3. Women's Thirst For Power Over Men Is The Pathway To Become A Garbage.* (Original work published 2013 in Russian, ISBN 9781301553075.). Marina Del Rey, CA: Catalog Of Human Souls GP. ISBN 9781301435500

Davydov, A., & Skorbatyuk, O. (2013). *A Log With Legs Spread Wide: Vol. 4. The Head – In The Underpants.* (Original work published 2013 in Russian, ISBN 9781301051281.). Marina Del Rey, CA: Catalog Of Human Souls GP.

Manipulative Games For Women

Davydov, A., & Skorbatyuk, O. (2013). *Manipulyativnyye Igry Dlya Zhenshchin* [Manipulative Games For Women]: *Vol. 1. March 23: Instruction for Exploitation of Men* (2nd ed., in Russian. Original work published 2005, Moscow: SNIALTotems. ISBN 9785716101333). Marina Del Rey, CA: Catalog Of Human Souls GP. ISBN 9781301803521

Davydov, A., & Skorbatyuk, O. (2013). *Manipulyativnyye Igry Dlya Zhenshchin* [Manipulative Games For Women]: *Vol. 2. April 6: Instruction for Exploitation of Men* (2nd ed., in Russian. Original work published 2005, Moscow: SNIALTotems. ISBN 9785716101302). Marina Del Rey, CA: Catalog Of Human Souls GP. ISBN 9781301069286

Davydov, A., & Skorbatyuk, O. (2013). *Manipulyativnyye Igry Dlya Zhenshchin* [Manipulative Games For Women]: *Vol. 3. October 13: Instruction for Exploitation of Men* (2nd ed., in Russian. Original work published 2005, Moscow: SNIALTotems. ISBN 9785716101326). Marina Del Rey, CA: Catalog Of Human Souls GP. ISBN 9781301900824

Davydov, A., & Skorbatyuk, O. (2013). *Manipulyativnyye Igry Dlya Zhenshchin* [Manipulative Games For Women]: *Vol. 4. December 7: Instruction for Exploitation of Men* (2nd ed., in Russian. Original work published 2005, Moscow: SNIALTotems. ISBN 9785716101319). Marina Del Rey, CA: Catalog Of Human Souls GP. ISBN 9781301413065

Secret Sexual Desires

Bazilevsky, K. (2013). *How To Seduce Men/Women Born On <Date> Or Secret Sexual Desires of 10 Million People: Demo From Shan Hai Jing Research Discoveries by A. Davydov & O. Skorbatyuk.* (Vols. 1-10). San Diego, CA: HPA Press.

Bazilevsky, K. (2013). *How To Seduce Men & Women Born On March 5 Or Secret Sexual Desires of 20 Million People: Demo From Shan Hai Jing Research Discoveries by A. Davydov & O. Skorbatyuk.* San Diego, CA: HPA Press. ISBN 9781301087204

Bazilevsky, K. (2013). *Secret Sexual Desires of 100 Million People— Seduction Recipes For Men & Women: Demos From Shan Hai Jing Research Discoveries by A. Davydov & O. Skorbatyuk.* San Diego, CA: HPA Press. ISBN 9780988648579 ISBN 9781301135035 ISBN 9780988648586

A list of other publications related to our scientific research can be found at http://www.humanpopulationacademy.org/publications/.

CONNECT WITH US

1. Visit our official website.

Human Population Academy and Special Scientific Info-Analytical Laboratory—Catalog of Human Souls:
http://www.HumanPopulationAcademy.org

2. Connect with us on social networks.

- ❖ *Facebook* - http://www.facebook.com/HumanPopulationAcademy (Note: you must be logged in to *Facebook* in order to access this page.)
- ❖ *YouTube* - http://www.youtube.com/user/HumanPopulAcademy
- ❖ *Google+* - http://plus.google.com/+HumanpopulationacademyOrghumannature
- ❖ *LinkedIn* - http://www.linkedin.com/company/2484433
- ❖ *Twitter* - http://twitter.com/HumanPopAcademy

3. Contact us.

The most reliable way to contact us is through CatalogOfHumanSouls profile on Amazon.com. You can find out how to do this step-by-step at the Human Population Academy's website under Contacts (http://www.humanpopulationacademy.org/breakthrough-discovery/contacts/).

However, this method might not be very convenient for those, who do not use Amazon.com. In this case, you can try to contact us by leaving a message on the website http://www.humanpopulationacademy.org (at the bottom of any page, where Leave a Reply form exists; for example, on the Contacts page). You can also try to contact us through social networks listed above. However, if you contacted us this way and did not get a response from us within two business days, we recommend that you send us a letter using Amazon.com.

ABOUT US

Special Scientific Info-Analytical Laboratory—Catalog of Human Souls was founded by Andrey Davydov. The laboratory is engaged in research and decryption of the ancient Chinese monument Shan Hai Jing, as well as other ancient texts, and creation of the *Catalog of human population*. The technology of uncovering individual structures of psyche of *Homo sapiens* for this Catalog was developed by Andrey Davydov; it is not based on any existing domestic or foreign research, methods or theoretical concepts. The laboratory is a partner with the Human Population Academy.

Human Population Academy was founded by Kate Bazilevsky. The Academy's mission is to inform all of over 7 billion humans living on Earth about the discovery of the *Catalog of human population*. The Academy educates about the *Catalog of human population* (*Catalog of Human Souls*) and provides access to informational materials from this Catalog to the public.

LEADERSHIP

ANDREY DAVYDOV

Research Supervisor of the Special Scientific Info-Analytical Laboratory—Catalog of Human Souls

Andrey Davydov is an expert in Chinese culture, researcher of ancient texts, the author of scientific discovery of the *Catalog of human population* and the technology of decryption of the ancient Chinese monument Shan Hai

Jing as the *Catalog of human population*. He authored over 300 published books, including scientific monographs and ideologies. In 2012, he was granted political asylum in the USA due to persecution by a group of employees of the Federal Security Service of Russian Federation (FSB, formerly KGB), who decided to expropriate his research product—the *Catalog of human population*.

OLGA SKORBATYUK

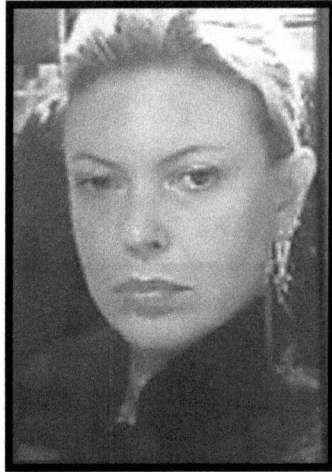

Senior Analyst at the Special Scientific Info-Analytical Laboratory—Catalog of Human Souls

Olga Skorbatyuk is a professional psychologist, one of the developers of the *Catalog of human population*, the founder of Non-Traditional Psychoanalysis, and co-author of over 300 books and scientific articles. She was granted political asylum in the USA together with A. Davydov.

KATE BAZILEVSKY

Founder of the Human Population Academy, Junior Analyst at the Special Scientific Info-Analytical Laboratory—Catalog of Human Souls

Kate Bazilevsky is the director of the Human Population Academy, a Junior Analyst at the Catalog of Human Souls laboratory, an author and a translator of books about the *Catalog of human population*. She holds a degree in MIS and psychology. She founded the Human Population Academy in 2011 and a publishing company called HPA Press in 2012.